NEW JERSEY
ADVENTURE BUCKET LIST

150+ MUST-SEE BEACHES, HIDDEN GEMS, ICONIC LANDMARKS, OUTDOOR ESCAPES, AND FAMILY FUN WITH INSIDER TIPS

BONUS VIDEO INSIDE

COLORED PHOTOS

DR. FANATOMY

copyright@ dr. fanatomy 2025

All rights reserved. No part of this publication may be reproduced, distributed, or transmitted in any form or by any means, including photocopying, recording, or other electronic or mechanical methods, without the prior written permission of the publisher, except in the case of brief quotations embodied in critical reviews and certain other noncommercial uses permitted by copyright law.

This book is a work of non-fiction, and any resemblance to actual persons, living or dead, or actual events is purely coincidental.

The information and techniques described in this book are intended for educational and informational purposes only. The author and publisher shall not be held liable for any injury, damage, or loss arising from using or misusing the information presented in this book.

While every effort has been made to ensure the accuracy of the information contained within this book, the author and publisher make no warranties or representations express or implied, about the completeness, accuracy, reliability, suitability, or availability with respect to the contents of this book for any purpose. The use of any information provided in this book is at the reader's own risk.

VIDEO : NEW JERSEY
Top 10 Instagrammable Locations

 https://youtu.be/C2Zgvzb_gTlk

OR

TABLE OF CONTENTS

1. INTRODUCTION: WHY NEW JERSEY SHOULD BE YOUR NEXT ADVENTURE
(Pg:4-9)

Unveiling New Jersey's True Charm
- A State of Surprises: Beaches, Forests, and Cities
- Historical Riches: Revolutionary War Sites and Industrial Landmarks
- Modern Marvels: Entertainment, Cuisine, and Culture

Fun Facts and Trivia About New Jersey
- The First Boardwalk and the Birthplace of Saltwater Taffy
- Home of Thomas Edison, Frank Sinatra, and Bruce Springsteen
- Unique Flora and Fauna in the Garden State

How to Use This Book
- Exploring by Region, City, or Interest
- Customizable Itineraries for All Types of Travelers
- Accessing the Interactive Map

2. RIDGE AND VALLEY: THE APPALACHIAN BEAUTY (Pg: 10-25)

Overview
- Location and Geography
- Best Time to Visit

Must-See Destinations
- Delaware Water Gap National Recreation Area
- High Point State Park (New Jersey's Highest Elevation)
- Buttermilk Falls and Sunfish Pond
- Historic Blairstown Village

Hidden Gems
- Lakota Wolf Preserve
- Peters Valley School of Craft

Activities
- Hiking, Birdwatching, and Photography

Sample Itineraries

3. HIGHLANDS: NEW JERSEY'S RUSTIC CHARM (Pg: 26-41)

Overview
- Geological Significance and Scenic Trails
- Perfect Getaway for Outdoor Enthusiasts

Must-See Destinations
- Lake Hopatcong and Surrounding Parks
- Ringwood State Park and Skylands Botanical Garden
- Morris Canal Greenway
- Sterling Hill Mining Museum

TABLE OF CONTENTS

Hidden Gems
- *Cooper Gristmill*
- *Hacklebarney State Park*
- *Activities*
- *Boating, Fishing, and Mine Tours*

Sample Itineraries

4. PIEDMONT: THE URBAN MEETS THE SUBURBAN (Pg: 42 - 54)

Overview
- Rolling Hills and Bustling Cities
- Cultural and Historic Highlights

Must-See Destinations
- Princeton University and Campus Tour
- Thomas Edison National Historical Park
- Red Mill Museum Village in Clinton
- Great Swamp National Wildlife Refuge

Hidden Gems
- Grounds for Sculpture in Hamilton
- Lambertville and Frenchtown (Art and Antique Lovers' Haven

Activities
- Museums, Art Tours, and Boutique Shopping

Sample Itineraries

5. ATLANTIC COASTAL PLAIN: BEACHES AND BEYOND

(Pg: 55-70)

Overview
- *Inner and Outer Coastal Regions*
- *A Paradise for Beach Lovers*

Must-See Destinations
- *Cape May (Historic Victorian Seaside Town)*
- *Atlantic City Boardwalk and Casinos*
- *Long Beach Island (LBI) and Barnegat Lighthouse*
- *Edwin B. Forsythe National Wildlife Refuge*

Hidden Gems
- *Sunset Beach (WWII Bunker and Cape May Diamonds)*
- *Ocean Grove's Great Auditorium*

Activities
- *Swimming, Fishing, and Historic Walking Tours*

Sample Itineraries

TABLE OF CONTENTS

6. GATEWAY REGION: URBAN ADVENTURES AND CULTURAL DELIGHTS

(Pg: 71 - 85)

- **Overview**
  - Northeastern Corner: Gateway to NYC and Beyond
  - Historic and Cultural Landmarks
- **Must-See Destinations**
  - Liberty State Park (Statue of Liberty Views)
  - Newark Museum of Art
  - New Jersey Performing Arts Center (NJPAC)
  - Branch Brook Park (Cherry Blossoms)
- **Hidden Gems**
  - Thomas Edison's Menlo Park Museum
  - Military Park in Newark
- **Activities**
  - Shopping, Theater, and Culinary Delights
- **Sample Itineraries**

7. THE ULTIMATE NEW JERSEY TRAVEL PLANNER-150 DESTINATIONS

(Pg: 86-96)

- Jersey Shore Getaway: Beaches, Boardwalks, and Family Fun (3 Days)
- Family-Friendly 5-Day Itinerary: Exploring New Jersey's Best Destinations
- Adventure and Nature Escapade: 5-Day Itinerary Across New Jersey
- History and Heritage Trail: 4-Day Journey Through New Jersey's Rich Past
- Nature's Escape: A 4-Day Adventure in New Jersey's Great Outdoors
- Cultural Gems and Historical Trails: A 3-Day Journey Through New Jersey's Heritage
- Nature Escapes and Outdoor Adventures: A 3-Day Expedition Through New Jersey's Wild Side
- Historic Gems and Cultural Highlights: A 3-Day Journey Through New Jersey's Rich Heritage
- Family-Friendly Adventures: A 3-Day Fun-Filled Itinerary in New Jersey
- New Jersey Hidden Gems: 3-Day Itinerary for Unique and Off-the-Beaten-Path Experiences

APPENDIX

(Pg: 97-101)

- Must-Visit Restaurants/Eating Places in New Jersey
- Family-Friendly 5-Day Itinerary: Exploring New Jersey's Best Destinations
- Must-Visit Kid-Friendly Sites in New Jersey
- Seasonal Festivals in New Jersey
- Best Seasonal Attractions for Families
- Top Historical Sites for Families in New Jersey
- Best Adventure Activities for Families

CONCLUSION

(Pg: 102)

1. The Garden State Awaits: Why New Jersey Should Be Your Next Adventure

Introduction

New Jersey, often overshadowed by its iconic neighbor, New York, is a vibrant tapestry woven with surprises. This **"Garden State"** boasts a diverse landscape, a rich history deeply intertwined with the birth of America, and a thriving modern culture that offers something for every traveler. Let this chapter be your guide, igniting your curiosity and showcasing why New Jersey deserves a prominent place on your travel bucket list.

Unveiling New Jersey's True Charm: A State of Surprises

From the sandy shores of the Atlantic coast to the rugged peaks of the Appalachian Mountains, New Jersey offers a remarkable diversity of landscapes.

Coastal Bliss:

- **Cape May:** This charming Victorian town boasts pristine beaches, elegant architecture, and a relaxed coastal vibe.

- **Atlantic City:** Experience the thrill of world-class casinos, vibrant nightlife, and a historic boardwalk, the first of its kind.

Natural Wonders :

- **Pine Barrens:** Explore this unique ecosystem with its vast pine forests, cranberry bogs, and opportunities for kayaking, hiking, and birdwatching.

- **High Point State Park:** Ascend to the highest point in New Jersey for breathtaking panoramic views of the surrounding countryside.

Urban Vibrancy:

- **Newark**: Immerse yourself in the city's rich history and vibrant arts scene, exploring museums, catching a performance at the renowned New Jersey Performing Arts Center, and indulging in diverse culinary experiences.

- **Jersey City:** Enjoy stunning skyline views of Manhattan, explore vibrant neighborhoods, and discover a thriving arts and cultural scene.

Atlantic City, New Jersey

Pine Barrens, New Jersey

By Famartin - Own work, CC BY-SA 4.0, https://commons.wikimedia.org/w/index.php?curid=35352569

By National Park Service - This file was derived from: Pinelands National Reserve LOC 2008620884.jpg, Public Domain, https://commons.wikimedia.org/w/index.php?curid=77953976

Historical Riches: A Legacy Forged in Revolution and Industry

New Jersey played a pivotal role in shaping American history, earning the moniker "Crossroads of the Revolution."

Revolutionary War Heritage:

- **Princeton Battlefield State Park**: Witness the site of a crucial turning point in the Revolutionary War.

- **Morristown National Historical Park**: Step back in time and explore George Washington's winter encampment during the harsh winter of 1779-1780.

Princeton Battlefield State Park
Daderot, CC BY-SA 3.0
<http://creativecommons.org/licenses/by-sa/3.0/>,
via Wikimedia Commons

Morristown National Historical Park
By Zeete - Own work, CC BY-SA 4.0,
https://commons.wikimedia.org/w/index.php?curid=127799575

Industrial Legacy:

- **Thomas Edison National Historical Park**: Delve into the life and work of the "Wizard of Menlo Park," exploring his laboratories and learning about his groundbreaking inventions.

- **Paterson Great Falls**: Witness the power of the Passaic River at these majestic falls, a testament to the state's early industrial might.

Modern Marvels: Entertainment, Cuisine, and Culture

New Jersey is a dynamic state with a thriving contemporary culture.

Entertainment:

- **Atlantic City**: Beyond the casinos, enjoy world-class entertainment, from live music and Broadway shows to exciting nightlife.

- **New Jersey Performing Arts Center (NJPAC)**: Experience a diverse range of performances, from classical music and dance to Broadway shows and contemporary music.

Culinary Delights:

- **Diner Culture**: Indulge in classic American diner fare, from juicy burgers and crispy fries to fluffy pancakes.

- **Seafood Specialties**: Savor fresh seafood at the Jersey Shore, including delectable oysters, clams, and crab.

- **The "Taylor Ham" or "Pork Roll" Debate**: Engage in the state's most beloved culinary debate – is it Taylor ham or pork roll?

Cultural Experiences:

- **Grounds for Sculpture**: Explore this unique outdoor museum featuring contemporary sculptures amidst serene gardens.

- **Diverse Festivals**: Experience the state's vibrant cultural scene through a variety of festivals celebrating everything from film and food to music and art.

Fun Facts and Trivia

- **Boardwalk Beginnings**: Atlantic City boasts the world's first boardwalk, built in 1870.
- **The Birthplace of Saltwater Taffy**: This iconic candy was invented in Atlantic City after a local candy shop was flooded with seawater in the late 1800s.
- **Home to Legends**: New Jersey is the birthplace of renowned figures including Thomas Edison, Frank Sinatra, and Bruce Springsteen.
- **A Unique Ecosystem**: The state is home to over 2,000 plant species, including the rare and delicate swamp pink.
- **Wildlife Encounters:** Observe diverse wildlife, including red foxes, great blue herons, and even bald eagles.

How to Use This Book

This book is your guide to exploring New Jersey's diverse offerings.

- **Regional Focus:** Navigate the state with ease through chapters dedicated to specific regions and cities.

- **Customized Itineraries:** Find inspiration with sample itineraries designed for various travel styles, from short-day trips to extended weekend getaways.

This chapter serves as your starting point for an unforgettable New Jersey adventure. Whether you're a first-time visitor or a lifelong resident, this book will unveil the Garden State's hidden treasures and inspire you to explore its diverse offerings.

2. Ridge and Valley : The Appalachian Beauty

The Ridge and Valley region of New Jersey, a captivating landscape of rolling hills, lush forests, and crystal-clear streams, beckons nature enthusiasts and adventure seekers alike. This scenic corner of the state, nestled in the northwestern region, offers a unique blend of iconic landmarks and hidden gems, showcasing the Garden State's rugged beauty.

Overview

Location and Geography: Situated in northwestern New Jersey, the Ridge and Valley region is characterized by the distinctive parallel ridges and valleys formed by the Appalachian Mountains. The Delaware River forms a significant portion of its eastern

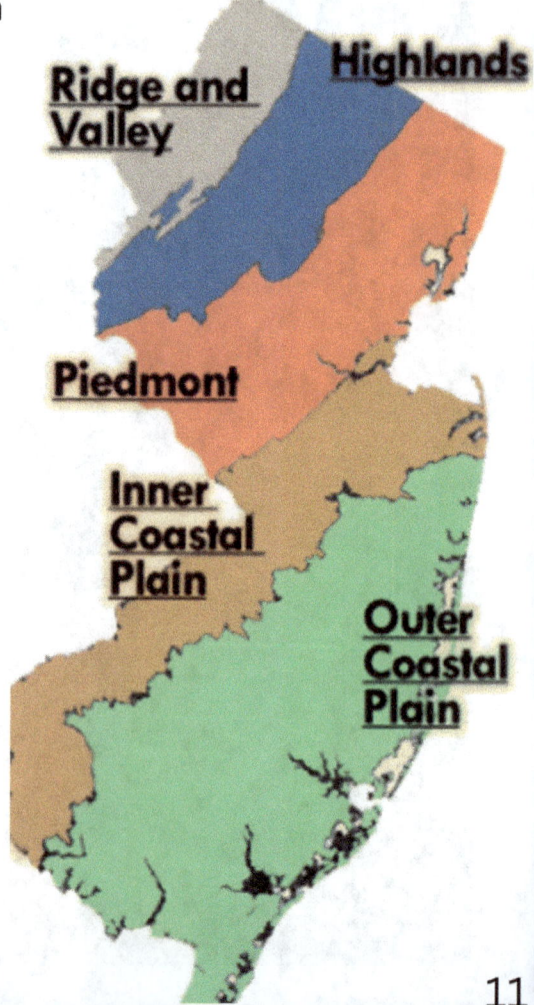

Key Features:

- **Rugged Terrain**: This region is renowned for its diverse topography, featuring rolling hills, deep valleys, and fast-flowing rivers, creating a paradise for outdoor enthusiasts.

- **Climate**: Experience four distinct seasons, with vibrant spring blooms, lush summer greenery, stunning fall foliage, and snowy winter landscapes.

- **Accessibility**: Easily accessible from major cities in New Jersey and neighboring states, making it a convenient destination for weekend getaways and longer vacations.

Best Time to Visit

- **Spring (April-May):** Witness the breathtaking display of wildflowers blooming across the hillsides. Enjoy mild temperatures perfect for hiking and exploring.

- **Summer (June-August):** Ideal for outdoor activities like hiking, kayaking, and camping. Embrace the warm weather and enjoy the vibrant summer scenery.

- **Fall (September-October):** Experience the breathtaking transformation of the foliage as the leaves turn vibrant shades of red, orange, and yellow.

- **Winter (November-March):** Enjoy the serenity of snow-covered landscapes. Explore the region on cross-country ski trails or snowshoe through the peaceful forests.

A) Must-See Destinations

Delaware Water Gap National Recreation Area

- **Highlights**: Hike along scenic trails with stunning views of the Delaware River, cascading waterfalls, and unique rock formations. Enjoy kayaking, canoeing, and fishing on the river.
- **Notable Trail**: Mount Tammany offers challenging but rewarding hikes with panoramic views of the Delaware Water Gap.

Silver Thread Falls, the smaller waterfall at Dingman's Falls site
Public Domain, https://commons.wikimedia.org/w/index.php?curid=97960844

Mount Tammany
By Nicholas . The original uploader was CPacker at English Wikipedia. - originally posted to Flickr as Kittatinny View, CC BY 2.0, https://commons.wikimedia.org/w/index.php?curid=4079173

Key Tips

Park Overview

- Located on the New Jersey and Pennsylvania border, featuring forested mountains, grassy beaches, and the iconic Delaware Water Gap.
- Offers miles of trails, including a section of the Appalachian Trail and Dingmans Creek Trail leading to Dingmans Falls.

Facilities and Activities

- Picnic tables available; grills allowed only in designated areas.
- Dogs are permitted but must be in approved areas.
- Swimming and other activities are restricted to specific zones—verify ahead of time.

Planning Ahead

- No food or supplies available for purchase within the park—pack all essentials, including plenty of drinking water and ice.
- Wear a life jacket near water and check for ticks during and after your visit.
- Check the park website, Facebook page, or call ahead for details on activities, hours, and regulations.

Avoiding Crowds

- Visit on weekdays (Tuesday–Thursday) to beat the crowds; weekends are the busiest.
- Arrive early (mornings or early evenings) for the best views and fewer visitors.
- Popular spots may reach capacity by 9 am on summer weekends—have backup plans in case your first-choice destination is full.

Exploring Less-Visited Areas

- With 70,000 acres, over 150 miles of trails, and 40 miles of river, explore beyond the popular trails at Mt. Minsi and Mt. Tammany or the waterfalls.
- Discover new favorite places by venturing into quieter sections of the park.

Travel Tips

- Coordinate plans with your group before arriving; cell service is limited in many areas.
- Stay together to ensure everyone can access your destination if parking areas reach capacity.

Recreation Guidelines

- Follow all park rules and regulations.
- Practice "Leave No Trace" principles: Plan ahead, minimize impact, respect wildlife, and pack out all trash and waste.
- Bring trash bags for cleanup and help keep the park pristine.

How to Reach Delaware Water Gap National Recreation Area

By Car
- From New York City: Take I-80 West. Travel time is approximately 1.5 to 2 hours, depending on traffic.
- From Philadelphia: Take I-476 North to I-80 West. Travel time is approximately 2 to 2.5 hours, depending on traffic.
- Parking: Popular parking areas include Kittatinny Point, Dunnfield Creek (NJ), and Milford Beach (PA). Arrive early, especially on weekends and holidays, as parking can fill up quickly.

By Public Transport
- From New York City: Martz Trailways offers bus service to the Delaware Water Gap Park & Ride in Pennsylvania, which is located near park entrances.
- Consider utilizing ride-sharing services or taxis from the Park & Ride to reach specific trailheads or destinations within the park.
- From Philadelphia: Take a bus to Stroudsburg, Pennsylvania.
- From Stroudsburg, use ride-sharing services (Uber/Lyft) or taxis to reach your desired location within the park.

By Air
- Nearest Airports: Newark Liberty International Airport (EWR): Located approximately 60 miles from the park.
- Lehigh Valley International Airport (ABE): Located approximately 45 miles from the park.
- Renting a car is highly recommended for easy access to various parts of the park and surrounding areas.

Tips
- Download Maps: Download offline maps and trail guides to your phone or a GPS device, as cell phone service can be unreliable in some areas of the park.
- Plan for Traffic: Be prepared for potential traffic delays, especially during peak seasons and weekends, particularly on I-80.
- Consider Mid-Week Visits: If possible, consider visiting during weekdays to avoid larger crowds and potential parking challenges.

High Point State Park

- **Significance:** As the highest point in New Jersey (1,803 feet), High Point State Park offers breathtaking panoramic views of New York, Pennsylvania, and even parts of three other states.

- **Activities:** Climb the iconic High Point Monument for panoramic vistas. Enjoy swimming in Lake Marcia, explore the park's extensive network of hiking trails, and camp under the stars.

Key Tips

Park Overview

High Point State Park

By AndyZ at en.wikipedia - Own workTransferred from en.wikipedia, Public Domain, https://commons.wikimedia.org/w/index.php?curid=17980977

- Located in Sussex County, New Jersey, High Point State Park boasts the state's highest elevation at 1,803 feet, offering breathtaking panoramic views of three states: New Jersey, New York, and Pennsylvania. The park features a diverse landscape of forested trails, scenic picnic areas, and the iconic High Point Monument, making it a popular destination for outdoor enthusiasts.

Facilities and Activities

- **Picnic Areas**: Enjoy designated picnic areas equipped with tables and grills for a relaxing outdoor meal.
- **Swimming**: Swimming is permitted in Lake Marcia during the summer season. Lifeguards are on duty during designated hours.
- **Hiking & Biking**: Explore over 50 miles of trails suitable for hiking, biking, and cross-country skiing in the winter.

Other Activities:

- **Fishing:** Enjoy fishing opportunities in Lake Marcia.
- **Birdwatching**: Observe a variety of bird species throughout the park.
- **Camping**: Campgrounds are available within the park for overnight stays. (Note: Reservations are often required, especially during peak season.)

Planning Ahead

- **Essentials:** Pack all necessary essentials, including water, snacks, sunscreen, insect repellent, and sturdy footwear for hiking.
- **Dress Appropriately:** Dress in layers to accommodate changing weather conditions.
- **Check Park Information:** Visit the official High Point State Park website or call the park office for the most up-to-date information on park hours, closures, and any special event announcements.

https://nj.gov/dep/parksandforests/parks/highpointstatepark.htmltext

How to Reach High Point State Park

By Car
- From New York City: Take I-80 West to NJ-23 North. Travel time is approximately 1.5 to 2 hours, depending on traffic.
- From Philadelphia: Take I-476 North to I-80 West, then I-80 East to NJ-23 North. Travel time is approximately 2 to 2.5 hours, depending on traffic.
- Parking: Main parking areas are located near the High Point Monument, Lake Marcia, and Steeny Kill Falls. Arrive early, especially on weekends and holidays, as parking can fill up quickly.

By Public Transport
- From New York City:Take NJ Transit trains or buses to Port Jervis, New York.
- From Port Jervis, utilize ride-sharing services (Uber/Lyft) or taxis to reach the park entrance. Travel time from Port Jervis to the park is approximately 15-20 minutes.
- From Newark or Jersey City:Take NJ Transit buses to Sussex, New Jersey.
- From Sussex, use ride-sharing services or taxis to reach the park entrance.

By Air
- Nearest Airports:Newark Liberty International Airport (EWR): Located approximately 65 miles from the park.
- Stewart International Airport (SWF): Located approximately 40 miles from the park.
- Renting a car is the most convenient option for accessing the park and exploring the surrounding areas.

Tips
- Cell Service: Cell phone reception may be limited within certain areas of the park. Download offline maps and trail guides to your phone or a GPS device before you arrive.
- Check Traffic Conditions: Check for real-time traffic updates on NJ-23, especially during peak travel times, to avoid potential delays.
- Plan for Peak Season: Be prepared for increased traffic and crowds during peak seasons, such as weekends, holidays, and summer months.

Buttermilk Falls and Sunfish Pond:

Buttermilk Falls: One of New Jersey's tallest waterfalls, cascading over a series of cliffs.

Key Tips for Visiting

Best Time to Visit

- **Spring:** Experience the most dramatic water flow as snowmelt feeds the falls.
- **Early Summer:** Enjoy lush greenery and comfortable temperatures for hiking.
- **Autumn:** Witness the stunning fall foliage as the leaves change colors.

Important Considerations

- **Footwear**: Wear sturdy hiking boots with good traction, as the trails near the falls can be steep, rocky, and slippery, especially when wet.
- **Essentials**: Bring plenty of water, snacks, and insect repellent, especially during the summer months. Don't forget your camera to capture the breathtaking scenery!
- **Respect Nature**: Stay on marked trails to protect the delicate ecosystem. Practice Leave No Trace principles by packing out all trash and minimizing your impact on the environment.

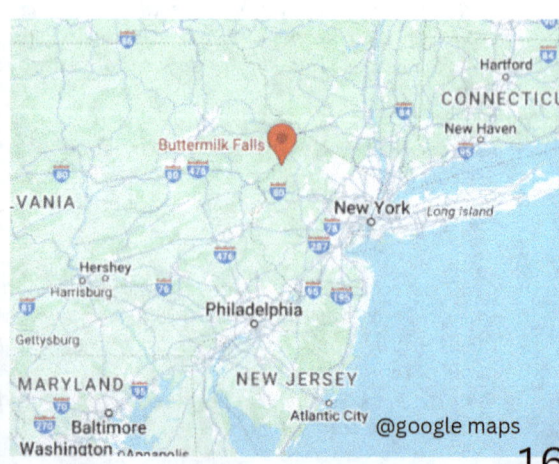

@google maps

16

How to Reach Buttermilk Falls

- **By Car:** Access Buttermilk Falls via Buttermilk Falls Road, which is accessible from NJ-206 or US-209.
- **Parking**: Limited parking is available near the falls. Arrive early, especially on weekends and during peak season, to secure a parking spot.
- **Nearest Landmarks**: Located in Walpack Township, Sussex County, New Jersey, near the Delaware Water Gap National Recreation Area.

What to See and Do

- **The Falls**: Marvel at the 200-foot cascading waterfall. You can view the falls from the base or climb the steep wooden staircase for a closer perspective.
- **Hiking**: Buttermilk Falls Trail: A short but moderate trail leads to the falls and connects to the Appalachian Trail (AT).
- **Blue Mountain Loop Trail:** A more challenging hike offering elevated views of the falls and the surrounding forests.
- **Wildlife Viewing**: Keep an eye out for native wildlife, such as birds (including woodpeckers and warblers), deer, and small mammals.

Sunfish Pond:

Sunfish Pond is a 44-acre glacial lake nestled in a 258-acre hardwood forest on the Kittatinny Ridge within Worthington State Forest. It is near the Delaware Water Gap National Recreation Area in Warren County, New Jersey. The Appalachian Trail passes along the lake's western and northern edges.

Key Tips for Visiting

Trail Preparation

- **Choose Your Route:** The most common route is via the Dunnfield Creek Trail (approximately 4.5 miles one-way), offering a moderate to strenuous hike. Alternatively, you can access Sunfish Pond via the Appalachian Trail (AT), which requires a longer hike.

Trail Preparation

- **Be Prepared:** Pack plenty of water, snacks, sunscreen, insect repellent, and layers of clothing to adapt to changing weather conditions.
- **Sturdy Footwear:** Wear sturdy hiking boots with good traction, as the trails can be rocky, uneven, and potentially muddy, especially after rain.

At the Pond

- **Enjoy the Scenery**: Relax and soak in the beauty of this pristine glacial lake. Sunfish Pond is a fantastic location for photography and peaceful reflection.
- **Picnic Spot**: Designated picnic areas are available around the pond. Enjoy a leisurely picnic and savor the tranquility of the surroundings.
- **Fishing**: Fishing is permitted in Sunfish Pond. Please check local regulations for any specific rules or restrictions.
- **Swimming Prohibited**: Swimming is prohibited in Sunfish Pond to protect the delicate aquatic ecosystem.

How to Reach Sunfish Pond

- **Trailheads:Dunnfield Creek Trailhead:** Located off I-80 at the Delaware Water Gap National Recreation Area.
- **Appalachian Trail Access**: Access the AT from the Kittatinny Valley State Park Visitor Center or Worthington State Forest.
- **By Car**: Use I-80 to reach the appropriate trailhead. Parking is available at designated areas.

Important Considerations

- **Check Weather Conditions**: Be aware of the weather forecast. Trails can become muddy and slippery after rain, and thunderstorms can occur unexpectedly.
- **Arrive Early**: Arrive early in the morning to avoid crowds, especially on weekends and during peak season.
- **Navigation**: Cell phone service can be unreliable within the park. Carry a detailed trail map and consider downloading offline maps to your GPS device.
- **Stay Hydrated**: Bring plenty of water and replenish your fluids throughout the hike.
- **Leave No Trace**: Practice Leave No Trace principles by packing out all trash, staying on marked trails, and minimizing your impact on the environment.

By Famartin - Own work, CC BY-SA 4.0, https://commons.wikimedia.org/w/index.php?curid=35284054

By Zeete - Own work, CC BY-SA 4.0, https://commons.wikimedia.org/w/index.php?curid=116905477

Sunfish Pond

Historic Blairstown Village:

- **What to See:** Explore the charming village with its quaint shops, historic buildings, and a classic small-town atmosphere.
- **Trivia**: Blairstown gained notoriety as the filming location for the iconic horror film "Friday the 13th."

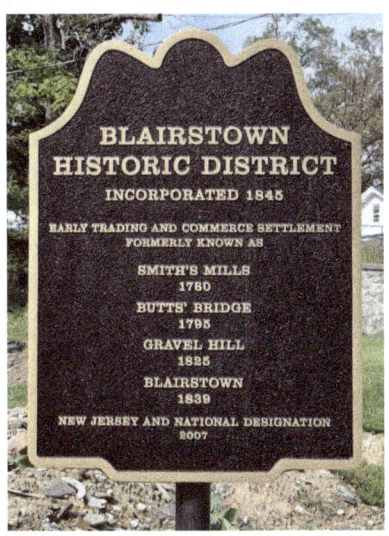
By Zeete - Own work, CC BY-SA 4.0, https://commons.wikimedia.org/w/index.php?curid=95028904

The Mill
By Zeete - Own work, CC BY-SA 4.0, https://commons.wikimedia.org/w/index.php?curid=95028904

How to Reach Historic Blairstown Village

By Car
- From New York City: Take I-80 West to NJ-94 North. Blairstown is about a 1.5-hour drive.
- From Philadelphia: Take I-476 North to I-80 East, then follow NJ-94 North. The drive takes approximately 2 hours.

Public Transportation
- Train & Bus: Take a NJ Transit train to Dover, NJ, and then a bus or rideshare to Blairstown. Public transit options may be limited, so confirm schedules in advance.

Best Times to Visit
- Spring & Summer: Perfect for enjoying the outdoor charm and events.
- Fall: The village is surrounded by stunning fall foliage.
- Halloween Season: Great time for fans of "Friday the 13th" to visit its filming locations.

Travel Tips
- **Dining**: Enjoy a meal at one of the local cafes or restaurants.
- **Parking**: Street parking is available, but it can fill up during busy weekends or events.
- **Weather Prep**: Wear comfortable shoes for walking and dress for the season.

B) Hidden Gems

Lakota Wolf Preserve:

- **Unique Experience:** Observe wolves, bobcats, and foxes in a naturalized setting.
- **Tours:** Participate in guided educational tours that provide insights into wolf behavior and wildlife conservation.

How to Reach

By Car

- **From New York City:** Take I-80 West towards the Delaware Water Gap. Follow signs to the specific wildlife center or conservation area hosting the tours.
- **From Philadelphia:** Use I-476 North to I-80 East. Look for local signage to the facility near the Delaware Water Gap area.

Public Transportation

- **Train & Rideshare:** Use NJ Transit to a nearby town, such as Blairstown or Stroudsburg, and take a rideshare or taxi to the wildlife center. Public transit may be limited, so plan accordingly.

Travel Tips

- **Family-Friendly:** Guided tours are often suitable for all ages, making them a great family outing.
- **Weather Prep:** Wildlife observation happens outdoors, so bring sunscreen, hats, or rain gear depending on the forecast.
- **Refreshments:** Bring water and light snacks if allowed, as tours can last an hour or more.
- **Accessibility:** Contact the facility in advance to confirm accessibility accommodations if needed.

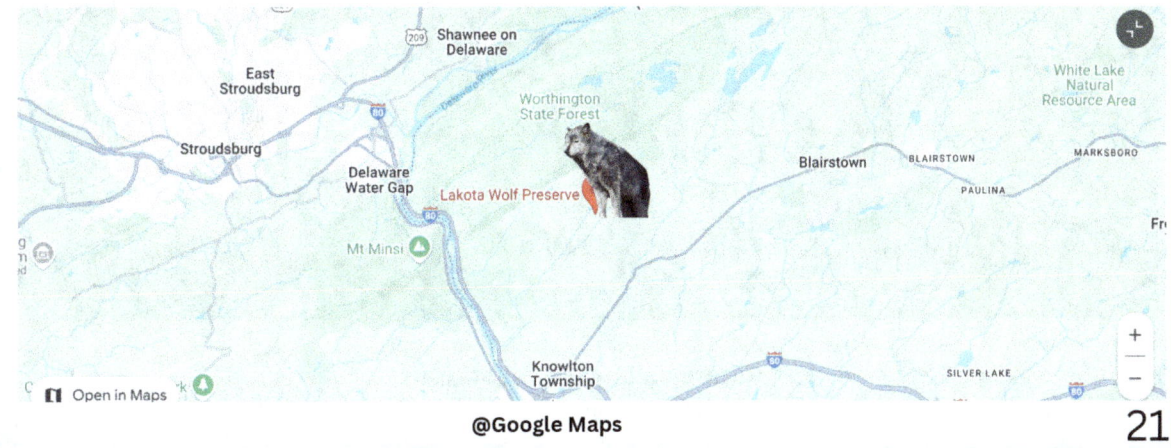

@Google Maps

Peters Valley School of Craft :

Plan Your Visit

- **Workshops:** Book your workshop in advance, as spaces fill quickly. Review the course catalog on the official website to choose the craft you'd like to explore.
- **Skill Levels:** Many workshops cater to beginners, but check the skill level requirements to ensure you pick one suitable for your experience.
- **Duration:** Workshops can range from a few hours to multiple days. Plan your visit accordingly if you're traveling from out of town.

What to Bring

- **Clothing:** Wear comfortable, casual clothes that can get dirty, and closed-toe shoes, especially for hands-on crafts like blacksmithing or ceramics.
- **Tools:** Check if tools or materials are provided. In some cases, you may need to bring your own or purchase them on-site.
- **Snacks and Water:** Bring light refreshments if allowed. There may be facilities on-site, but options can be limited during busy periods.

Peters Valley School of Craft
By Zeete - Own work, CC BY-SA 4.0, https://commons.wikimedia.org/w/index.php?curid=112421879

Travel Tips

- **Seasonal Visits:** Workshops and galleries are most active during spring, summer, and fall. Check the schedule to align your visit with your interests.
- **Family-Friendly:** Many activities are suitable for all ages, but confirm age restrictions for workshops.
- **Accessibility:** Contact the school in advance to inquire about accessibility options for individuals with mobility challenges.
- **Extend Your Trip:** Peters Valley is located near the Delaware Water Gap National Recreation Area, making it an excellent addition to a day or weekend trip exploring nature and art.

Activities in Ridge & Valley Region

Hiking

Trail Name	Details	Best Time to Visit
Rattlesnake Swamp Trail	Easy trail with boardwalks and opportunities for birdwatching.	Spring and Fall for cooler temperatures and scenic views.
Stairway to Heaven	Challenging climb with breathtaking views of the surrounding landscape.	Spring and Fall for comfortable weather and clear views.

Birdwatching

Location	Details	Best Time to Visit
Kittatinny Valley State Park	A haven for diverse bird species, including bald eagles and red-tailed hawks.	Early mornings in Spring and Summer.
Flatbrook-Roy Wildlife Area	Excellent diversity of songbirds and other species in a serene natural setting.	Early mornings in Spring and Summer.

Photography

Spot	Details	Best Time to Visit
Delaware Water Gap Overlooks	Panoramic views of the river and valleys, ideal for capturing landscapes.	Early mornings and late afternoons for optimal lighting.
High Point Monument	Iconic location for sunrises and sunsets with expansive vistas.	Early mornings and evenings for vibrant hues.

Sample Itenaries

1-Day Adventure Itinerary

Time	Activity	Details
Morning	Hike at High Point State Park and visit the High Point Monument	Climb the iconic monument for panoramic views of New Jersey, Pennsylvania, and New York.
Afternoon	Visit Peters Valley School of Craft	Explore art galleries, witness artisans at work, and enjoy hands-on craft workshops.
Evening	Scenic drive along the Delaware Water Gap	Stop at overlooks like Kittatinny Point Visitor Center for breathtaking views of the river and valleys.

3-Day Exploration Itinerary

Day	Activity	Details
Day 1	Hike a section of the Appalachian Trail	Enjoy serene forest views and camp overnight near Sunfish Pond, a glacial lake with tranquil surroundings.
Day 2	Visit Buttermilk Falls and Historic Blairstown Village	Admire one of NJ's tallest waterfalls, followed by shopping and dining in the quaint Blairstown Village.
Day 3	Morning at Lakota Wolf Preserve; Afternoon kayaking or fishing on the Delaware River	Observe wolves in their habitat, then relax with water activities on the scenic river.

Family-Friendly Getaway Itinerary

Time	Activity	Details
Morning	Guided tour at Lakota Wolf Preserve	Learn about wolf behavior and wildlife conservation through interactive tours.
Afternoon	Hike to Buttermilk Falls and enjoy a picnic lunch	A short, family-friendly trail leads to the cascading waterfall, perfect for a leisurely lunch.
Evening	Ice cream and stroll in Blairstown	Treat the family to local ice cream and explore the village's historic charm.

Adventure-Seeker's Weekend Itinerary

Day	Activity	Details
Day 1	Kayak through the Delaware Water Gap	Paddle through scenic stretches of the river, navigating gentle currents and enjoying nature.
Day 2	Hike the Stairway to Heaven trail	Challenge yourself on steep climbs and be rewarded with sweeping views from the summit.
Day 3	Camp at High Point State Park	Spend the night under the stars, enjoying the peace of the wilderness and a campfire.

Relaxation Retreat Itinerary

Day	Activity	Details
Day 1	Scenic drive along Route 521	Enjoy rolling hills, farmlands, and photo-worthy landscapes. Stop at picturesque viewpoints along the way.
Day 2	Relax at Sunfish Pond	Unwind by the serene glacial lake, perfect for reflection, photography, or a peaceful walk.
Evening	Dinner at a farm-to-table restaurant	Savor fresh, locally sourced meals at a regional gem.

3. Highlands: New Jersey's Rustic Charm

Overview

The Highlands region of New Jersey offers a captivating blend of natural beauty, historical sites, and outdoor recreation. This picturesque region, characterized by rolling hills, forested valleys, and sparkling lakes, provides a welcome escape from the hustle and bustle of city life.

Geological Significance and Scenic Trails :

The Highlands region boasts a rich geological history, shaped by ancient volcanic activity and glacial movements. This unique geological past has resulted in stunning landscapes, including cascading waterfalls, deep gorges, and scenic vistas. The region is crisscrossed by a network of hiking trails, offering opportunities for all levels of experience, from leisurely strolls to challenging treks.

A) Must-See Destinations

Lake Hopatcong and Surrounding Parks:

New Jersey's largest lake, Lake Hopatcong, offers a variety of recreational activities, including boating, fishing, and swimming. Explore the surrounding parks, such as Hopatcong State Park, for picnicking, hiking, and enjoying the lake views.

Tips for Visiting Lake Hopatcong and Surrounding Areas

Lake Hopatcong is a jewel in New Jersey's Highlands, offering a mix of recreational activities, historic sites, and scenic beauty. Whether you're visiting for the day or planning a weekend retreat, these tips and an itinerary will help you make the most of your trip.

- **Watersports:** Rent equipment like kayaks, paddleboards, or wakeboards at one of the many marinas around the lake. **Pro Tip**: Early mornings offer the calmest waters for kayaking and paddleboarding.

- **Fishing:** Lake Hopatcong is a fishing paradise. Target largemouth bass with plastic worms or crankbaits, and try tube jigs for smallmouth bass. **Best Spots**: Focus on shaded areas or near docks for the best catch.

- **Hiking & Biking**: Hopatcong State Park offers excellent trails for all fitness levels. **Resource**: Check AllTrails for reviews and maps to match your hiking experience.

- **Dining**: Lakeside restaurants like Stone Water and The Jefferson House provide stunning views and delicious meals. **Don't Miss**: Try the seafood specials while enjoying the sunset over the lake.

- **Museum Visit**: Dive into the area's history at the Lake Hopatcong Historical Museum. **Highlight:** Learn about the Morris Canal and Native American history.

Seasonal Fun:
- **Summer**: Swim at Mount Arlington Municipal Beach or enjoy picnics in the parks.
- **Winter:** Try ice boating or ice fishing for a unique experience.

How to Reach Lake Hopatcong

Lake Hopatcong is easily accessible from various locations in New Jersey and neighboring states. Here's a guide to help you plan your trip:

By Car

From New York City (Approx. 1 hour, 40 miles):

- *Take I-80 West.*
- *Exit at Route 15 North toward Jefferson/Sparta.*
- *Follow signs to Lake Hopatcong or Hopatcong State Park.*

From Philadelphia (Approx. 1 hour 45 minutes, 90 miles):
- *Take I-95 North.*
- *Merge onto I-287 North toward Morristown.*
- *Exit to I-80 West, then Route 15 North to Lake Hopatcong.*

From Newark Liberty International Airport (Approx. 45 minutes, 40 miles):
- Take I-78 West to I-287 North.
- Merge onto I-80 West and follow Route 15 North.

Parking:
- Free parking is available at Hopatcong State Park and Mount Arlington Municipal Beach.
- Some marinas and restaurants also offer parking for patrons.

By Train
- Take NJ Transit's Morris & Essex Line to Lake Hopatcong Station.
    - Trains run frequently from New York Penn Station and Newark Broad Street.
    - Travel Time: About 1.5 hours from New York Penn Station.
    - From the station: Use a rideshare app (Uber/Lyft) or a local taxi to reach the lake (5–10 minutes).

By Bus
- NJ Transit Bus Route 880: Connects nearby towns to Lake Hopatcong.
    - Check the schedule on the NJ Transit website for timings and stops.

By Air
- Nearest Airports:
    - Newark Liberty International Airport (EWR): Approximately 45 miles.
    - Morristown Municipal Airport: Approximately 25 miles for private and charter flights.
- From the airport, rent a car or use a rideshare service to reach the lake.

Lake Hopatcong State Park
Tomwsulcer, CC0, via Wikimedia Commons

Ringwood State Park and Skylands Botanical Garden

Explore the historic Ringwood Manor and its surrounding parklands. Visit the Skylands Botanical Garden, featuring a diverse collection of plants and stunning views.

Tips for Visiting Ringwood State Park and Skylands Botanical Garden

Admission and Fees:
- Free garden admission before Memorial Day; $5 parking fee afterward.
- New Jersey residents aged 62+ can get a free pass at the park office.

Picnic Areas:
- No picnics or barbecues in the Skylands section. Use Ringwood Manor or Shepherd Lake picnic areas instead.

Pack Smart:
- Bring trash bags for cleanup, as there are no trash receptacles.
- Carry water and comfortable walking shoes for trails and garden exploration.

Seasonal Beauty:
- Visit year-round to experience seasonal changes in the garden and surrounding woods.

Trail Options:
- Try the 1.5-mile loop trail for a scenic hike or walk. Dogs are welcome on a leash.

Explore the Garden:
- Discover specialty areas like the crabapple vista, terraced gardens, perennial beds, and woodland paths.
- Look for unique plants such as Japanese umbrella pine, Atlas cedar, and European beech.

Self-Guided Tours:
- Use the self-guided tour brochure to learn about the plants and garden history.

Plan Your Visit:
- Allocate 2–3 hours to explore. Enjoy views of the Ramapo Mountains and visit nearby manors.

How to Reach Ringwood State Park and Skylands Botanical Garden

By Car:
- *From NYC: Take I-80 W, merge onto I-287 N, and exit 55 for Wanaque/Ringwood. Follow signs to the park.*
- *From Newark: Take I-280 W, merge onto I-287 N, and follow the same exit route.*

By Public Transit:
- *Take NJ Transit's Main/Bergen-Port Jervis Line to Sloatsburg Station. From there, use a taxi or rideshare to reach the park (approx. 15 minutes).*

Parking:
- *Available at the park and garden entrance. Fees apply during peak seasons.*

Tips for Travel:
- *Arrive early on weekends or holidays to secure parking.*
- *Use GPS: Enter "Skylands Manor" for precise navigation.*

Skylands, Ringwood
Zeete, CC BY-SA 4.0 <https://creativecommons.org/licenses/by-sa/4.0>, via Wikimedia Commons

Morris Canal Greenway

Hike or bike along the historic Morris Canal Greenway, a linear park following the route of the former canal. Enjoy scenic views and discover remnants of the region's industrial past.

Morris Canal
By Zeete - Own work, CC BY-SA 4.0, https://commons.wikimedia.org/w/index.php?curid=72406292

Tips for Visiting Morris Canal Greenway

Overview and Significance:
- The Greenway traces the historic Morris Canal, once vital for transporting coal and goods in the 19th century.
- t spans over 102 miles through six counties in New Jersey, offering scenic trails and historical sites.

Trail Options:
- Sections range from short paved paths to rugged hiking trails. Popular areas include Waterloo Village, Wharton, and Ledgewood.
- Ideal for walking, biking, and light hiking.

Historical Highlights:
- Visit restored canal locks, inclines, and historic villages along the route.
- Explore interpretive signage that details the canal's engineering marvels and cultural significance.

Seasonal Exploration:
- Best visited in spring or fall for comfortable weather and colorful foliage.
- Winter offers serene landscapes and opportunities for photography.

Family-Friendly Stops:
- Waterloo Village: A historic canal town with restored buildings and educational tours.
- Ledgewood Basin: Features a preserved lock and canal store with exhibits.

What to Bring:
- Comfortable walking shoes or a bike for exploring the trails.
- A reusable water bottle and snacks, as amenities are limited along some sections.
- A camera or phone to capture scenic views and historical landmarks.

Plan Ahead:
- Check trail maps and conditions on the official Morris Canal Greenway website or apps like AllTrails.
- Many sections are pet-friendly but require leashes.

How to Reach Morris Canal Greenway

- **By Car:**
  - Waterloo Village: From NYC, take I-80 W, exit 25 to Route 206 N. From Newark, use I-280 W to I-80 W.
  - Ledgewood Basin: Follow Route 46 to Ledgewood and look for canal signage.
- **By Public Transit:**
  - Take NJ Transit's Dover Train Line to a nearby station, then use a taxi or rideshare.
- **Parking:**
  - Available at Waterloo Village and Wharton Canal Park; some areas may charge a small fee.
- **Tips:**
  - Use GPS for directions, and plan extra time to explore the historical and scenic stops.

Sterling Hill Mining Museum

Hike or bike along the historic Morris Canal Greenway, a linear park following the route of the former canal. Enjoy scenic views and discover remnants of the region's industrial past.

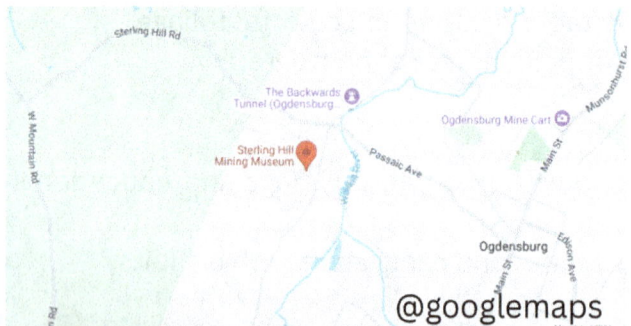
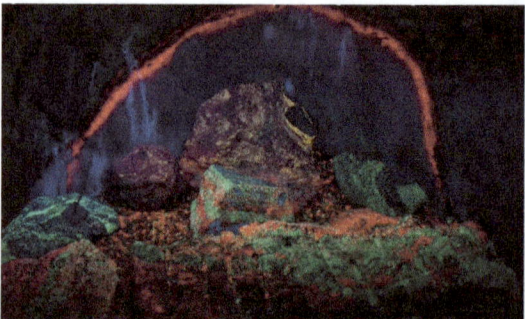

The Rainbow Room

Sterling Hill Mining Museum

Tips for Visiting

- **Take a Guided Tour:** Explore the mine's tunnels while learning about its history, geology, and unique fluorescent minerals.
- **Wear Comfortable Shoes:** The tour involves walking on uneven surfaces, so sturdy footwear is recommended.
- **Dress for the Weather:** Underground temperatures remain cool year-round; bring a light jacket, even in summer.
- **Visit the Museum Store:** Browse unique mineral specimens and mining-related souvenirs.
- **Plan Ahead:** Check the official website for tour times and any special events.

How to Reach Sterling Hill Mining Museum

By Car:
- **From NYC**: Take I-80 W, exit 34B to NJ-15 N, and follow signs to Ogdensburg.
- **From Newark**: Use I-280 W to I-80 W, then exit 34B to NJ-15 N.

By Public Transit:
- Take NJ Transit to Dover or Hackettstown stations, and then use a taxi or rideshare to reach the museum.

Parking:
- Free on-site parking is available.

B)Hidden Gems

Cooper Gristmill

Visit this beautifully preserved 19th-century gristmill to learn about the region's agricultural heritage.

Take a Guided Tour:
- Guided tours are the best way to understand the history of the gristmill and see the water-powered machinery in action.
- Learn about how grain was ground in the 19th century and the mill's role in the community.

Explore Nearby Trails:
- The mill connects to scenic hiking trails like the Patriots' Path and Black River Trail, perfect for nature enthusiasts.
- The trails offer opportunities to spot wildlife and enjoy the tranquil surroundings.

Visit During Special Events:
- The mill hosts events like milling demonstrations, historical reenactments, and seasonal activities for families.
- Look for craft-making workshops and historical storytelling sessions.

Dress Comfortably:
- Wear sturdy shoes, especially if you plan to explore the nearby trails or walk around the grounds.

Pack Snacks or a Picnic:
- There are picnic areas near the Black River where you can enjoy a meal amidst beautiful scenery.
- Remember to carry your trash out, as it's a carry-in, carry-out location.

Photography:
- The mill and surrounding areas are picturesque. Bring a camera or smartphone to capture historic structures, the river, and lush greenery.

Check Hours and Accessibility:
- The mill operates seasonally, typically from spring to fall. Check their official website or call ahead for hours.
- The facility is family-friendly, but not all areas are wheelchair accessible, so inquire about accessibility options if needed.

How to Reach Cooper Gristmill

By Car:

From New York City:
- Take I-78 W towards New Jersey.
- Exit 29 to merge onto I-287 N.
- Take Exit 30B for NJ-202 N toward Bernardsville/Chester.
- Continue on NJ-202 N, turn left onto County Road 513/Main Street in Chester, and follow signs to the gristmill.

From Newark:
- Take I-280 W and merge onto I-80 W.
- Exit 27A for US-206 S toward Somerville.
- Turn right onto County Road 513/Main Street, and follow the signs to the gristmill.

By Public Transit:
- Take NJ Transit's Morris & Essex Line to Morristown station.
- From Morristown, use a taxi, rideshare service, or local bus to reach Chester and the Cooper Gristmill.

Parking:
- Free parking is available on-site.
- During peak seasons or special events, additional parking may be available nearby with directional signs.

Cooper Grist Mill Water Wheel

Fourpenguins, CC BY-SA 3.0 <https://creativecommons.org/licenses/by-sa/3.0>, via Wikimedia Commons

Hacklebarney State Park

Explore this scenic park featuring cascading waterfalls, rugged cliffs, and hiking trails.

- The park's centerpiece, the Black River, offers stunning views, especially during fall when the foliage transforms into vibrant hues.
- Trails along the river can be rocky and uneven, so wear sturdy footwear.

Tips for Visiting Hacklebarney State Park

Hiking Options:
- The park has 3.7 miles of trails, mostly easy and suitable for beginners or families.
- Along the river, trails are rougher with roots and rocks, adding a bit of adventure.
- Trails are ideal for quick hikes, beginner hikers, and families with children due to shorter distances and easy access.
- For shorter routes, consult trail maps or follow signage to minimize backtracking.

Nearby Attractions:
- Combine your visit with nearby spots like Schooley's Mountain, Kay's Cottage Ruins, Black River-Cooper Mill, Voorhees State Park, or Columbia Trail.
- Don't miss Hacklebarney Cider Mill, just minutes away, for cider, donuts, and other fall treats.

Picnic Perfect:
- The park is dotted with numerous picnic tables, making it an ideal spot for a meal amidst nature.
- Bring your own food and enjoy a peaceful outdoor dining experience.

Accessibility:
- Many trails feature paved or gravel sections, ensuring easier access for those looking for a relaxed outing.

How to Reach Hacklebarney State Park

By Car:
- **From New York City:**
    - Take I-78 W to NJ-24 W.
    - Merge onto I-287 S.
    - Exit 22B for US-202/US-206 N toward Bedminster/Netcong.
    - Follow signs to County Road 513 S and then County Road 517 to Hacklebarney State Park.

- **From Newark:**
    - Take I-280 W and merge onto I-80 W.
    - Exit 27A for US-206 S.
    - Continue onto County Road 513 S and then County Road 517 to the park entrance.

By Public Transit:
- Take NJ Transit's Morris & Essex Line to Chester or Gladstone.
- From the station, use a taxi or rideshare service to reach the park.

Parking:
- Free parking is available at the main entrance.
- Arrive early to secure a spot, especially during weekends or peak seasons.

Travel Tips:
- Use GPS with "Hacklebarney State Park" for precise directions.
- Allocate at least 2-3 hours for a leisurely visit, including hiking and a picnic.
- Visit in fall for the most picturesque experience and stop by Hacklebarney Cider Mill for a perfect seasonal treat.

Black River waterfalls

By Zeete - Kaugalingong trabaho, CC BY-SA 4.0, https://commons.wikimedia.org/w/index.php?curid=108290978

Sample Activities

Category	Activities
Outdoor Recreation	Boating and Fishing: Enjoy boating and fishing on Lake Hopatcong or other area lakes.
Outdoor Recreation	Hiking and Biking: Explore the region's extensive network of hiking and biking trails.
Outdoor Recreation	Horseback Riding: Several stables offer horseback riding opportunities through scenic trails.
Historical & Cultural	Museum Visits: Visit the Sterling Hill Mining Museum to delve into the region's mining history.
Historical & Cultural	Historic Sites: Explore Ringwood Manor and other historic landmarks for a glimpse into the past.

Sample Itineraries: 1-Day Itinerary: History and Nature

Time of Day	Activity	Details
Morning	Visit Sterling Hill Mining Museum	Learn about the region's mining history.
Afternoon	Hike at Hacklebarney State Park	Explore scenic trails and enjoy the picturesque waterfalls.

3-Day Itinerary: Lake Life and Canal Exploration

Day	Activity	Details
Day 1	Explore Lake Hopatcong	Rent a boat and spend the day enjoying the lake's beauty.
Day 2	Hike or bike along Morris Canal Greenway	Stop at historic sites along the way for a cultural experience.
Day 3	Relax and visit Skylands Botanical Garden	Spend the morning by the lake, then explore the gardens.

Family-Friendly Itinerary

Time of Day	Activity	Details
Morning	Visit Ringwood Manor and Skylands Botanical Garden	Enjoy historical insights and explore beautiful gardens.
Afternoon	Picnic and playground fun	Relax at Ringwood State Park and let kids enjoy the playground.
Evening	Tour Cooper Gristmill	Discover how grain was processed in the past.

Young Explorers Itinerary

Time of Day	Activity	Details
Morning	Fossil hunting at Sterling Hill Mining Museum	Engage kids with exciting hands-on fossil exploration.
Afternoon	Short, easy hike	Explore a local park with trails suited for beginners.

Romantic Getaway Itinerary

Activity	Details
Scenic picnic	Enjoy a private lunch at a secluded spot along the Morris Canal Greenway.
Sunset boat ride	Take a romantic boat ride on Lake Hopatcong and marvel at the sunset views.

4. Piedmont : The Urban Meets the Suburban

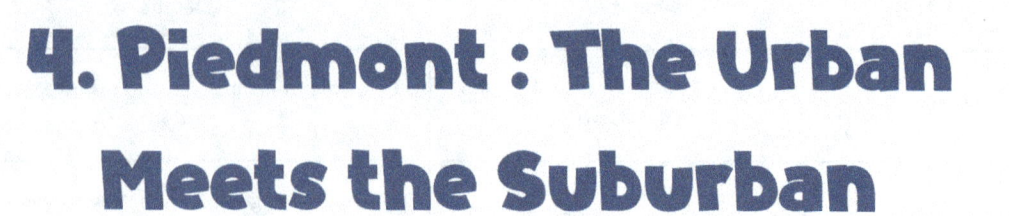

Piedmont: Where History Meets Innovation

The Piedmont region of New Jersey offers a captivating blend of rolling hills, vibrant cities, and charming towns. It's an ideal destination for those seeking a balance between urban energy and suburban tranquility. This chapter explores the region's must-see destinations, hidden gems, and exciting activities, providing curated itineraries to help you plan your perfect Piedmont adventure.

Overview: A Tapestry of History and Innovation

The Piedmont region boasts a rich tapestry of history and innovation. From the hallowed halls of Princeton University to the groundbreaking inventions of Thomas Edison, the Piedmont offers something for everyone. Explore scenic drives through rolling countryside, delve into the cultural buzz of cities like Princeton and Trenton, or immerse yourself in the natural beauty of the Great Swamp National Wildlife Refuge.

A) Must-See Destinations

Princeton University and Campus Tour:

- **Immerse yourself in history:** Founded in 1746, Princeton University is one of the most prestigious universities in the U.S. Explore its iconic Gothic architecture, including Nassau Hall, the Princeton University Art Museum, and serene Lake Carnegie.

- **Fun Fact:** Did you know Albert Einstein, one of the greatest minds of the 20th century, lived and worked in Princeton for over 20 years? You might even spot a future Nobel laureate strolling through the campus!

Tips for Visiting

- **Book a Guided Tour**
    - Reserve a campus tour online ahead of time, especially during peak seasons such as spring and fall. Guided tours provide fascinating insights into the university's history and architecture.

- **Plan for Parking**
    - Parking in Princeton can be challenging. Use the designated visitor parking lots or consider public transportation options.

- **Explore Beyond the Campus**
    - Take time to explore Princeton's charming downtown area, filled with cafes, bookstores, and boutique shops.

- **Best Times to Visit**
    - Spring and fall offer the most picturesque views, with blooming flowers or vibrant autumn foliage accentuating the campus beauty.

How to Reach Princeton University

Mode of Transport	Details
By Car	Princeton University is easily accessible from major highways, including I-95 and Route 1. Use "Visitor Parking Lot" for GPS.
By Train	Take an NJ Transit train to Princeton Junction, then transfer to the "Dinky," a short train ride to campus.
By Bus	NJ Transit buses connect Princeton to nearby cities like New Brunswick and Trenton.
By Air	The nearest airport is Trenton-Mercer Airport (about 15 miles away) or Newark Liberty International Airport (about 40 miles away).

Thomas Edison National Historical Park:

- **Step back in time**: Explore the laboratory and home of Thomas Edison, the "Wizard of Menlo Park," who revolutionized the world with inventions like the light bulb and the phonograph.

- **Interactive Exhibits**: Witness Edison's original inventions firsthand and participate in engaging demonstrations to understand the impact of his work.

- **Fun Fact:** Thomas Edison held over 1,000 patents in his lifetime, making him one of the most prolific inventors in history. His laboratory at this site was one of the first to adopt teamwork as an essential element of innovation—a precursor to modern research and development labs.

Thomas Edison's Laboratory

By Jim.henderson - Own work, CC0, https://commons.wikimedia.org/w/index.php?curid=15455497

Glenmont, Edison's estate

By VitaleBaby (talk) (Uploads) - Own work, Public Domain, https://commons.wikimedia.org/w/index.php?curid=49782000

Practical Tips for Visiting

Plan for Special Events

Weekends often feature living history demonstrations and special events that bring Edison's legacy to life. Check the park's website for schedules.

Take a Guided Tour
- Guided tours provide in-depth insights into Edison's work and personal life, including a walkthrough of his home, Glenmont. Book your tour online or at the visitor center upon arrival.

Arrive Early
- The park can get crowded during peak hours. Arriving early ensures you have ample time to explore both the laboratory complex and Glenmont.

Accessibility
- The main buildings are wheelchair accessible, and the staff can assist with additional accommodations if needed.

Photography
- While photography is allowed in most areas, some exhibits might restrict flash photography. Be sure to capture the essence of this historic location for memories!

How to Reach Thomas Edison National Historical Park

Mode of Transport	Details
By Car	The park is located at 211 Main Street, West Orange, NJ. Use "Thomas Edison National Historical Park" for GPS navigation. Parking is available on-site.
By Public Transit	Take NJ Transit's Morris & Essex Line to Orange Station, then use a local taxi or rideshare to reach the park (about 2 miles).
By Air	Newark Liberty International Airport is about 13 miles away. From there, use a rental car or rideshare service.

Sample Itenary

Time	Activity
10:00 AM	Arrive at the park and start with a tour of Edison's Laboratory Complex, exploring interactive exhibits.
12:30 PM	Break for lunch at a nearby café or picnic area.
1:30 PM	Tour Glenmont, Edison's Victorian-era home, and learn about his personal life and family.
3:00 PM	Participate in a live demonstration or special weekend event.
4:30 PM	Visit the museum shop for souvenirs and educational materials before departure.

Red Mill Museum Village in Clinton: A Window into New Jersey's Rural Pastk:

A Picturesque Escape: Nestled on the banks of the Raritan River in the charming town of Clinton, the Red Mill Museum Village is a celebrated icon of New Jersey's rural history. The village is home to a beautifully restored 19th-century gristmill and a collection of historic buildings that offer a deep dive into the state's agricultural and industrial heritage. Visitors can explore exhibits showcasing traditional crafts, tools, and farming equipment, providing a vivid picture of life in bygone eras.

Fall Foliage Spectacle : Plan your visit in the autumn, when the surrounding landscape transforms into a brilliant tapestry of red, orange, and gold hues. The Red Mill Museum Village becomes a haven for photographers and nature lovers during this season. Strolling along the riverbank, you'll find breathtaking views that perfectly capture the beauty of New Jersey's countryside.

By Zeete - Own work, CC BY-SA 4.0, https://commons.wikimedia.org/w/index.php?curid=103753533

By Zeete - Own work, CC BY-SA 4.0, https://commons.wikimedia.org/w/index.php?curid=102826061

Highlights and Experiences

Attraction	Description
The Red Mill	This 200-year-old gristmill is the centerpiece of the museum. Visitors can see the original grinding stones and machinery.
Historic Buildings	Includes a schoolhouse, carriage shed, and a log cabin—all offering insights into 18th- and 19th-century life.
Special Exhibits	Rotating displays on regional crafts, local history, and traditional farming methods.
Blacksmith Demonstrations	Watch live demonstrations of blacksmithing, showcasing traditional techniques.
Raritan River Views	Enjoy the stunning views of the river and the picturesque landscape, perfect for photography.

Practical Tips for Visiting

Plan Ahead
- Check the museum's website for seasonal hours, ticket prices, and special events such as craft fairs and historical reenactments.

Best Times to Visit
- Fall is the most picturesque season, but spring also offers pleasant weather and vibrant greenery. Weekdays are typically less crowded than weekends.

Interactive Tours
- Book a guided tour to gain in-depth knowledge about the mill's history and its role in the local economy.

Family-Friendly Activities
- The village frequently hosts family-friendly events such as holiday festivals and scavenger hunts, making it an excellent destination for kids.

Accessibility
- While some buildings may have uneven flooring due to their historic nature, most areas are accessible for visitors with mobility challenges.

How to Reach the Red Mill Museum Village

Mode of Transport	Details
By Car	Located at 56 Main Street, Clinton, NJ. Easily accessible from I-78. Free parking is available nearby.
By Public Transit	NJ Transit buses stop in Clinton; from there, the museum is a short walk.
By Air	The nearest airport is Newark Liberty International Airport (about 50 miles). Rent a car or use a rideshare service for the drive.

Sample Itineraries - 1-Day: Historical Immersion

Time	Activity
10:00 AM	Arrive at the Red Mill Museum Village and explore the gristmill.
12:00 PM	Take a leisurely stroll along the Raritan River and enjoy a picnic lunch.
2:00 PM	Tour the historic buildings and watch a blacksmith demonstration.
4:00 PM	Visit the gift shop for unique crafts and souvenirs.

Family-Friendly Day Trip

Time	Activity
10:00 AM	Explore the Red Mill and participate in a scavenger hunt for kids.
12:00 PM	Enjoy lunch at a family-friendly café in downtown Clinton.
2:00 PM	Visit the log cabin and schoolhouse for a fun, interactive history lesson.

Great Swamp National Wildlife Refuge: A Tranquil Retreat for Nature Enthusiasts:

Nestled in Morris County, New Jersey, the Great Swamp National Wildlife Refuge spans over 7,700 acres of wetlands, forests, and meadows. Established in 1960, this refuge is a sanctuary for wildlife and a peaceful retreat for nature lovers. With its diverse ecosystems and carefully maintained trails, the refuge offers opportunities to connect with nature, whether you're birdwatching, hiking, or simply enjoying the serene landscape

Highlights and Activities

Attraction	Description
Boardwalk Trails	Meander through lush wetlands and observe wildlife up close without disturbing their natural habitat.
Observation Platforms	Ideal for spotting birds and other wildlife, with panoramic views of the refuge.
Wildlife Observation	Encounter over 200 bird species, mammals like deer and foxes, amphibians, and reptiles.
Educational Programs	Participate in ranger-led tours and educational workshops focused on conservation and ecology.

Birdwatching at Its Best : The Great Swamp National Wildlife Refuge is a paradise for birdwatchers, with a rich variety of species throughout the year.

Season	Bird Species to Spot
Spring	Warblers, American woodcocks, and osprey during migration.
Summer	Blue herons, great egrets, and red-winged blackbirds nesting in the wetlands.
Fall	Migratory flocks of Canada geese and ducks, as well as bald eagles.
Winter	Northern harriers, owls, and woodpeckers can often be seen in the quieter months.

Tips for a Great Visit

Pack Essentials
- Bring binoculars, a camera, water, and snacks. Sturdy, comfortable shoes are a must for hiking the trails.

Plan Around the Seasons
- Spring and fall are ideal for birdwatching due to migration patterns. Summer offers lush greenery, while winter provides a quieter, serene experience.

Respect Wildlife
- Follow the "Leave No Trace" principles to preserve the refuge's natural beauty. Maintain a safe distance from all animals.

Visit the Helen C. Fenske Visitor Center
- Stop by the visitor center for maps, educational exhibits, and information on upcoming events.

Join Guided Tours
- Enhance your visit with ranger-led tours that delve into the refuge's unique ecosystems and conservation efforts.

Sample Itineraries

1-Day: Nature Immersion

Time	Activity
9:00 AM	Start at the Helen C. Fenske Visitor Center to learn about the refuge.
10:00 AM	Walk the boardwalk trail and enjoy birdwatching from observation platforms.
12:30 PM	Have a picnic lunch at a designated area.
2:00 PM	Join a ranger-led tour or hike the wildlife observation trails.
4:00 PM	Visit the observation blinds for late-afternoon birdwatching.

Family-Friendly Adventure

Time	Activity
10:00 AM	Take the kids on the easy-access boardwalk trail for a close look at nature.
11:30 AM	Participate in a family-friendly workshop at the visitor center.
1:00 PM	Enjoy lunch at a picnic spot while spotting wildlife from a distance.
2:30 PM	Finish the day with a scavenger hunt to identify native plants and animals.

How to Reach the Great Swamp National Wildlife Refuge

Mode of Transport	Details
By Car	Located in Morris County, NJ, the refuge is accessible via Route 287 and Route 24. Parking is free at multiple trailheads.
By Public Transit	NJ Transit trains and buses connect to nearby towns; from there, a short taxi or rideshare trip is required.
By Air	Newark Liberty International Airport is about 30 miles away. Rent a car or use rideshare services for the drive.

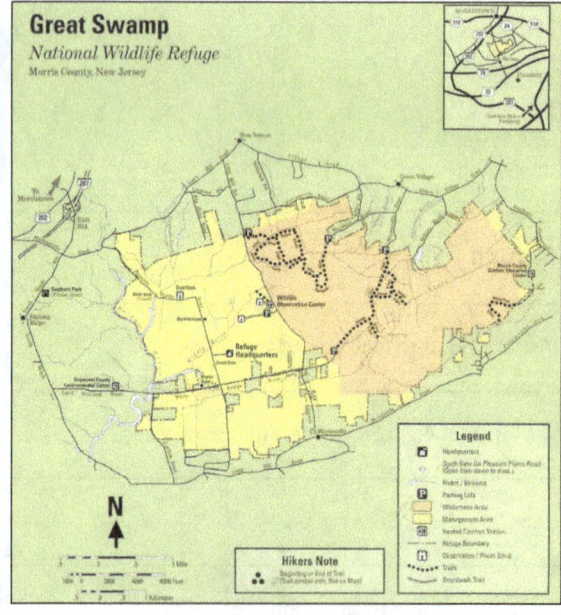

By U.S. Fish and Wildlife Service - http://www.fws.gov/northeast/greatswamp/map.pdf, Public Domain, https://commons.wikimedia.org/w/index.php?curid=4849727

By Jesper Rautell Balle - Own work, CC BY 3.0, https://commons.wikimedia.org/w/index.php?curid=3957897

Hidden Gems

Grounds for Sculpture in Hamilton:

- **Art in the open air:** Unleash your inner child at this whimsical sculpture park showcasing a diverse collection of works by renowned local and international artists. Explore larger-than-life installations, including Seward Johnson's iconic "Walking to Work" sculptures.
- **Unleash your creativity**: Participate in interactive art workshops or guided tours to gain a deeper appreciation for the sculptures and the creative process.

Lambertville and Frenchtown:

- **A haven for art and antiques**: Nestled along the Delaware River, these charming towns are a paradise for art and antique enthusiasts. Browse unique finds at the numerous antique shops, savor a delicious meal at a riverside cafe, or lose yourself amidst the vibrant art galleries showcasing local talent.
- **Fun Fact**: Lambertville is affectionately known as the "Antiques Capital of New Jersey," attracting collectors and treasure hunters from all over the region.

Activities

- **Immerse yourself in history and innovation**: Explore the museums and historical sites, including Princeton University, Thomas Edison National Historical Park, and the Red Mill Museum Village.
- **Embrace your artistic side**: Take a curated art tour at Grounds for Sculpture, browse the galleries in Lambertville and Frenchtown, or participate in an art workshop.
- **Treat yourself to retail therapy**: Discover unique treasures at the antique shops and boutiques in Frenchtown and Clinton.
- **Connect with nature**: Hike the peaceful trails at the Great Swamp National Wildlife Refuge, or take a relaxing stroll along the scenic boardwalk trails.

Sample Itineraries at a Glance

Itinerary	Morning	Afternoon
1-Day: A Walk Through Time	Princeton University: Explore Nassau Hall and the Art Museum.	Thomas Edison National Historical Park: Learn about Edison's inventions.
3-Day: Piedmont's Diversity		
Day 1	Hike at Great Swamp National Wildlife Refuge.	Visit Thomas Edison National Historical Park.
Day 2	Explore Lambertville and Frenchtown's shops and galleries.	Picnic along the Delaware River.
Day 3	Visit the Red Mill Museum Village in Clinton.	Relax in the picturesque countryside.
Family-Friendly	Red Mill Museum Village: Interactive exhibits and outdoor activities.	Browse shops and dine in Lambertville or Frenchtown.
Art Enthusiasts	Lambertville: Explore art galleries and antique shops.	Grounds for Sculpture: Contemporary art and serene park setting.
Nature Lovers	Scenic hike at Great Swamp National Wildlife Refuge.	Boardwalk trails: Observe wetland tranquility and abundant birdlife.

Tips for Planning Your Trip

Tip	Details
Check Seasonal Events	Look for local festivals, concerts, and farmers' markets to enhance your visit.
Consider the Season	Visit in spring for wildflowers or autumn for vibrant fall foliage.
Book Accommodations Early	Reserve ahead during peak seasons, weekends, or holidays.
Embrace Local Flavors	Try local restaurants and farm-to-table establishments for a culinary treat.
Support Local Businesses	Shop at boutiques, art galleries, and farmers' markets to boost the local economy.

5. Atlantic Coastal Plain: Beaches and Beyond

Atlantic Coastal Plain: Beaches and Beyond

Overview

The Atlantic Coastal Plain of New Jersey stretches from Sandy Hook in the north to Cape May in the south. This vibrant region offers a delightful blend of sandy beaches, charming historic towns, and a plethora of family-friendly activities. The Atlantic Coastal Plain can be further divided into two distinct regions:

- **Inner Coastal Plain**: Characterized by rolling hills, forests, wetlands, and barrier islands. Popular for birdwatching, hiking, and eco-tours.
- **Outer Coastal Plain**: Renowned for its pristine beaches, barrier islands, and iconic boardwalks. Ideal for swimming, sunbathing, surfing, and enjoying classic seaside entertainment.

(A) Must-See Destinations

Inner Coastal Region

Edwin B. Forsythe National Wildlife Refuge: A Natural Haven

The Edwin B. Forsythe National Wildlife Refuge spans over 47,000 acres of preserved wetlands, forests, and coastal habitats. It serves as a sanctuary for a vast range of wildlife, making it a premier destination for birdwatchers, nature enthusiasts, and families seeking outdoor adventures.

By Hornbaker Chelsi, U.S. Fish and Wildlife Service - http://www.public-domain-image.com/public-domain-images-pictures-free-stock-photos/nature-landscapes-public-domain-images-pictures/beaches-public-domain-images-pictures/holgate-beach-bulkhead.jpg, Public Domain, https://commons.wikimedia.org/w/index.php?curid=24893883

Feature	Details
Total Area	47,000 acres
Bird Species	Over 300, including ospreys, snowy egrets, blue herons, and migrating shorebirds
Key Habitats	Salt marshes, freshwater wetlands, upland forests, and tidal creeks
Seasonal Highlights	Spring and fall migrations bring an influx of birds along the Atlantic Flyway, a key migratory route.

What Makes It Unique?

- **Migratory Bird Hotspot**: The refuge is part of the Atlantic Flyway, a major route for migratory birds.
- **Eco-Diversity**: Offers a mix of salt marshes, tidal flats, and forested areas, supporting a wide variety of species.
- **Accessibility**: Family-friendly trails and boardwalks allow visitors of all ages to explore its beauty.

Birdwatching Highlights

Bird Species	Best Viewing Season	Habitats
Ospreys	Spring to early fall	Nesting platforms in marshes
Snowy Egrets	Spring to summer	Salt marshes and wetlands
Blue Herons	Year-round	Shallow water and marshes
Warblers	Spring migration	Forested uplands

Activities for Families and Nature Enthusiasts

Activity	Details
Guided Wildlife Tours	Led by experienced park rangers, these tours provide insights into the local flora and fauna.
Self-Guided Birdwatching	Explore at your own pace using maps and birding checklists provided at the visitor center.
Photography	Capture stunning views of marsh landscapes and close-ups of wildlife.
Hiking and Boardwalk Trails	Enjoy trails like the Wildlife Drive or the Songbird Trail, ideal for all skill levels.

Sample Itineraries

Itinerary	Details
Half-Day Visit	- Start with the Wildlife Drive to explore the refuge by car.
	- Stop at the Songbird Trail for a short hike and birdwatching.
1-Day Adventure	- Morning: Take a guided wildlife tour for expert insights.
	- Afternoon: Explore the Leeds Eco-Trail and enjoy a picnic lunch near the visitor center.

How to Reach Edwin B. Forsythe National Wildlife Refuge

Mode of Transport	Details
By Car	- From Atlantic City: U.S. Route 30 West → Great Creek Road- From Philadelphia: Atlantic City Expressway → Garden State Parkway (Exit 41)- From NYC: Garden State Parkway (Exit 48)
By Public Transport	- Train: NJ Transit to Absecon Train Station (4 miles from refuge)- Bus: NJ Transit buses to Absecon/Galloway Township (limited local access)
By Air	- Nearest Airport: Atlantic City International Airport (ACY), 10 miles from the refuge.- From ACY: Rent a car or take a taxi/rideshare.

Outer Coastal Region

Cape May: A Victorian Seaside Town (Established in 1769)

Cape May, established in 1769, is America's oldest seaside resort and a National Historic Landmark, famed for its Victorian architecture, pristine beaches, and cultural attractions.

Quick Facts

- **Cape May Lighthouse (1859)**: Second-oldest operating lighthouse in the U.S.
- **Cape May County Zoo**: Free entry with over 550 animals.
- **Bird Migration Hotspot**: A top location for fall birdwatching.
- **Cape May-Lewes Ferry:** Offers scenic rides across the Delaware Bay.

Highlights

- Stroll along streets lined with colorful gingerbread houses.
- Relax on award-winning beaches.
- Visit historical sites like the Emlen Physick Estate and the World War II Lookout Tower.

Cape May is a unique blend of history, relaxation, and natural beauty for all ages.

By Smallbones - Own work, CC0, https://commons.wikimedia.org/w/index.php?curid=26730404

Tips for Visiting Cape May

- **Best Time to Visit:** Late spring to early fall offers the best weather for beach activities and exploring.
- **Parking**: Free parking is available at the Cape May County Zoo; downtown Cape May has metered and free parking options.
- **Walking-Friendly**: The town is compact, making it ideal for walking tours. Rent bicycles for a more leisurely exploration.
- **Book in Advance**: Victorian inns and beachfront hotels fill up quickly, especially during summer weekends.
- **Dress Comfortably**: Wear light clothing and sunscreen, and bring a camera for the picturesque views from the lighthouse.
- **Family-Friendly**: The Cape May County Zoo and nearby beaches are great options for children and adults alike.

Sample Itinerary

Time	Activity
Morning	Start with a visit to the Cape May Lighthouse, climbing to the top for breathtaking ocean views.
Mid-Morning	Explore the streets of Cape May, admiring the Victorian architecture and stopping at local boutiques.
Lunch	Dine at a beachfront restaurant, enjoying fresh seafood and ocean views.
Afternoon	Spend time at the Cape May County Zoo, followed by a relaxing walk along the promenade or beach.
Evening	End the day with a sunset ferry ride or a classic Cape May carriage tour to soak in the town's charm.

How to Reach Cape May: Compact Guide

- By Car: Drive via the Garden State Parkway (Exit 0); ample parking is available near beaches and landmarks.
- By Train & Bus: Take NJ Transit trains to Atlantic City and connect via NJ Transit buses to Cape May.
- By Ferry: Enjoy scenic views aboard the Cape May-Lewes Ferry from Lewes, Delaware.
- By Air: The nearest airport is Atlantic City International (approximately 45 miles away), with shuttle or rental car options available.

Atlantic City Boardwalk and Casinos

Atlantic City's Boardwalk is a symbol of American leisure and entertainment, offering a blend of historic charm and modern excitement. Established in 1870 as the first boardwalk in the world, it stretches 4 miles along the Atlantic Ocean, providing visitors with unmatched scenic views, entertainment, and cultural experiences. Known for its bustling casinos, family-friendly attractions, and vibrant nightlife, Atlantic City remains a prime destination for travelers of all ages.

Fascinating Facts

- **Historic Landmark:** Built in 1870, the Atlantic City Boardwalk was initially designed to keep sand out of hotel lobbies.
- **Longest Running Attraction:** Steel Pier, first opened in 1898, still thrills visitors with rides and games.
- **Pop Culture Icon:** The Monopoly board game is based on Atlantic City street names.
- **World-Famous Casinos:** Atlantic City is home to iconic casinos like Borgata, Caesars, and Tropicana.

By Tim Emerich - https://www.publicdomainpictures.net/en/view-image.php?image=51396&picture=atlantic-city-boardwalk, CC0, https://commons.wikimedia.org/w/index.php?curid=88255826

Tips for Visiting

- **Family-Friendly Fun**: Visit during the day to enjoy Steel Pier rides, arcade games, and beachfront activities.
- **Best Time to Go**: Early morning and evening strolls offer cooler temperatures and stunning ocean views.
- **Pack Smart**: Comfortable walking shoes are a must for exploring the boardwalk.
- **Know the Rules:** Casino entry is restricted to those aged 21 and above.
- **Budget Wisely**: Look out for special discounts on boardwalk attractions and eateries.

How to Reach Atlantic City

Mode	Details
By Car	Drive via Garden State Parkway (Exit 38); multiple parking options nearby.
By Train	Take NJ Transit's Atlantic City Line, connecting from Philadelphia.
By Bus	Greyhound and NJ Transit buses directly serve the Atlantic City Terminal.
By Air	Atlantic City International Airport (12 miles away); shuttles and taxis available.

Sample Itineraries

1-Day Itinerary: Iconic Boardwalk Experience

- **Morning:** Stroll along the boardwalk, enjoy breakfast at a seaside café, and explore the Atlantic City Historical Museum.
- **Afternoon:** Visit Steel Pier for amusement rides and games. Enjoy lunch at a classic boardwalk eatery.
- **Evening:** Try your luck at a casino and catch a live performance or show.

Long Beach Island (LBI) and Barnegat Lighthouse

Long Beach Island (LBI), a 18-mile barrier island along the Jersey Shore, offers a serene escape with its pristine beaches, charming coastal towns, and historic landmarks. A key attraction, Barnegat Lighthouse, or "Old Barney," stands as a beacon of history and adventure, drawing visitors for breathtaking views and family-friendly activities.

Facts

Fact	Details
Barnegat Lighthouse height	172 feet
Construction date of Barnegat Lighthouse	1859
LBI length	18 miles
Number of towns on LBI	6 major municipalities, including Beach Haven and Surf City
Annual visitors to Barnegat Lighthouse	Over 500,000

Barnegat Lighthouse in Barnegat Light, Long Beach Island, New Jersey.
By Andrew Bossi - Own work, CC BY-SA 3.0, https://commons.wikimedia.org/w/index.php?curid=749809

Activities

Beach Fun and Relaxation
- Enjoy LBI's tranquil beaches, ideal for swimming, sunbathing, and family picnics.
- Tip: Visit Ship Bottom Beach or Surf City Beach for calm waters and clean sands.

Climb Barnegat Lighthouse
- Ascend 217 steps to the top of "Old Barney" for panoramic views of the Atlantic Ocean and Barnegat Bay.
- Fun Fact: The lighthouse was designed to guide ships away from dangerous shoals near the coast.

Cycling Along LBI's Path
- Rent bikes and explore the island's scenic bike path.
- Tip: The 18-mile path passes through quaint towns, making it perfect for family exploration.

How to Reach

Mode	Details
By Car	Drive via Route 72 E; LBI is approximately 1.5 hours from Philadelphia and 2 hours from New York City.
By Public Transit	NJ Transit provides bus services to Manahawkin, followed by a taxi or rideshare to LBI.

Sample Itinerary

1-Day Itinerary: Beaches and Lighthouse Adventure

Morning
Start the day with a beachside breakfast in Surf City.
Spend time at Ship Bottom Beach, enjoying sunbathing and shell collecting.

Afternoon

- Head to Barnegat Lighthouse State Park and climb to the top for stunning coastal views.
- Enjoy a picnic lunch overlooking Barnegat Bay.

Evening

- Rent bikes and explore the charming towns along LBI's 18-mile bike path.
- Wrap up the day with dinner at a local seafood restaurant, savoring fresh catch-of-the-day dishes.

B) Hidden Gems

Sunset Beach: WWII Bunker and Cape May Diamonds

Sunset Beach, located at the southern tip of Cape May, New Jersey, offers a perfect blend of history, natural beauty, and family-friendly activities. Famous for its stunning sunsets, this beach is home to the mysterious remnants of a WWII bunker visible offshore, as well as the unique "Cape May Diamonds" — quartz pebbles polished smooth by the Delaware Bay.

Facts & What to See

Feature	Details
Location	Cape May Point, New Jersey
Famous For	WWII concrete bunker and Cape May Diamonds
Sunset Views	One of the best spots on the East Coast to view breathtaking sunsets
Cape May Diamonds	Quartz crystals that resemble gemstones, found along the beach

Top Attractions

WWII Bunker
- Built during World War II as part of the harbor defense system.
- Visible at low tide, offering a glimpse into military history.

Cape May Diamonds
- Collect sparkling quartz crystals on the beach, a fun activity for all ages.
- Often polished and set into jewelry as souvenirs.

Flag Ceremony
- A daily patriotic ceremony conducted at sunset from May to September.

Tips for Visiting

- **Best Time to Visit:**
    - Evening hours for the iconic sunset.
    - Spring or summer for the best Cape May Diamond hunting.
- **Activities for Families:**
    - Bring a sieve or small shovel for kids to dig for Cape May Diamonds.
    - Explore the gift shops offering Cape May Diamond jewelry and other souvenirs.
- **Dining Nearby:**
    - Grab a meal at the Sunset Grill, offering casual seaside dining.
- **Photography Tip:**
    - The golden hour at Sunset Beach is perfect for capturing silhouettes against the colorful sky.

How to Reach Sunset Beach

Mode	Details
By Car	Drive along Sunset Boulevard, which leads directly to the beach. Parking is free.
By Public Transit	Public buses from Cape May City may run seasonally; a car is recommended for convenience.
Nearest Airport	Atlantic City International Airport (ACY), approximately 45 miles away.

Sample Itinerary: Sunset Beach

1-Day Hidden Gem Adventure

Morning
- Arrive early and enjoy a serene walk along the beach.
- Hunt for Cape May Diamonds along the shoreline.

Afternoon
- Visit the WWII bunker at low tide for a closer look at this historic structure.
- Shop for souvenirs at the Sunset Beach gift shop.

Evening
- Witness the daily flag ceremony.
- Relax and watch the sun set over the Delaware Bay, creating a picture-perfect end to your day.

World War II- Lookout Tower

World War II Bunker

Ocean Grove's Great Auditorium

Ocean Grove, a quaint Victorian town along the Jersey Shore, is home to the Great Auditorium — an architectural marvel built in 1894. Known for its immense wooden structure and superb acoustics, the auditorium remains a hub for cultural, religious, and musical events. Surrounding the auditorium, Ocean Grove offers charming streets lined with gingerbread-style homes, making it a delightful destination for families, architecture lovers, and history enthusiasts.

Facts & What to See

Feature	Details
Built	1894
Architectural Style	Victorian-era wooden structure with a soaring 6,000-seat capacity
Famous For	Organ concerts, choir performances, and community events
Nearby Attractions	Asbury Park Boardwalk, Victorian homes, and beaches

Top Attractions

The Great Auditorium
- Attend a concert or event to experience its legendary acoustics.
- Explore its rich history through exhibits and guided tours.

Tent City
- Adjacent to the auditorium, these unique seasonal tents are a remnant of Ocean Grove's camp meeting days.

Ocean Grove Beach
- A family-friendly beach with calm waters and a relaxed atmosphere.

Tips for Visiting

- **Best Time to Visit:**
    - Summer for events, concerts, and vibrant town activities.
- **Cultural Experience:**
    - Check the schedule for choir festivals, classical music concerts, and organ recitals.
- **Dining Nearby:**
    - Enjoy local eateries like Nagles Apothecary Café for a vintage dining experience.
- **Parking Tip:**
    - Parking can be limited; consider arriving early or using nearby public transport.

How to Reach Ocean Grove

Mode	Details
By Car	Accessible via Route 71 or Garden State Parkway. Street parking is available.
By Train	NJ Transit North Jersey Coast Line to Asbury Park, followed by a short walk or cab ride.
Nearest Airport	Newark Liberty International Airport (EWR), approximately 50 miles away.

Sample Itinerary: Ocean Grove's Great Auditorium

Time	Activities
Morning	- Stroll around Tent City, appreciating the charm of seasonal cottages.
Morning	- Take a guided tour of the Great Auditorium to explore its rich history.
Afternoon	- Enjoy lunch at a nearby café.
Afternoon	- Relax on Ocean Grove Beach and explore Victorian homes along Main Avenue.
Evening	- Attend a concert or event at the Great Auditorium to experience its phenomenal acoustics.

Activities and Sample Itineraries

Category	Details
Activities	Swimming: Enjoy pristine beaches along the Atlantic Coastal Plain, ideal for family outings.
	Fishing: Cast a line at popular fishing spots like Cape May or Barnegat Bay.
	Historic Walking Tours: Explore Victorian-era streets in Cape May or the iconic Atlantic City Boardwalk.

Sample Itinerary	Details
1-Day Itinerary	Morning: Take a walking tour in Atlantic City or Cape May, exploring history and architecture.
	Afternoon: Relax at a local beach or enjoy lunch at a seaside café.
	Evening: Visit a historic site or attend a live event.
3-Day Itinerary	Day 1: Explore Cape May's Victorian homes and Lighthouse.
	Day 2: Relax on Long Beach Island's beaches; visit Barnegat Lighthouse.
	Day 3: Take a nature walk or birdwatching tour at Edwin B. Forsythe Wildlife Refuge.
Family-Friendly Itinerary	Morning: Visit Cape May County Zoo or Barnegat Lighthouse.
	Afternoon: Explore the wildlife refuge and enjoy a picnic.
	Evening: Relax at a family-friendly beach or boardwalk.
Adventure-Seeker Itinerary	Morning: Try surfing lessons at Long Beach Island or kayaking in Barnegat Bay.
	Afternoon: Explore the island's scenic bike trails or nature spots.
	Evening: Watch the sunset or attend a local event.
Relaxation Itinerary	Morning: Enjoy the serenity of Sunset Beach with its unique Cape May Diamonds.
	Afternoon: Unwind at a Victorian inn or spa in Cape May.
	Evening: Savor a gourmet dinner with ocean views.

6. Gateway Region: Urban Adventures and Cultural Delights

Gateway Region: Urban Adventures and Cultural Delights

The Gateway Region in New Jersey is a dynamic mix of history, culture, and urban excitement. Situated in the northeastern corner of the state, this area serves as a gateway to New York City while offering its own distinct attractions and experiences. Whether you're a history buff, an art lover, or a foodie, the Gateway Region promises a variety of urban adventures and cultural delights.

Overview: A Strategic Location Steeped in History

The Gateway Region's strategic location, with Newark Penn Station offering easy access to New York City, makes it a popular choice for day trips and weekend getaways. Bustling cities like Newark, Jersey City, and Hoboken each contribute to the region's unique character. From its pivotal role in the Industrial Revolution to its thriving contemporary art scene, the Gateway Region has played a significant role in shaping both New Jersey and the United States. Visitors can delve into a diverse range of landmarks that showcase this rich history and vibrant culture.

(A) Must-See Destinations :

Liberty State Park:
Highlights

- **Breathtaking Views**: Get unparalleled vistas of the Statue of Liberty, Ellis Island, and the Manhattan skyline, perfect for photos or quiet reflection.
- **Ferry Access**: Direct ferries operate to the Statue of Liberty and Ellis Island. Pro tip: Ferry tickets can be purchased online to avoid long lines, and early morning departures are less crowded.
- **Liberty Science Center**: Just a short walk from the park, this center offers interactive exhibits and the largest planetarium in the Western Hemisphere.

Liberty State Park (LSP) is a scenic park in Jersey City, New Jersey, situated along Upper New York Bay. It lies directly across from Liberty Island and Ellis Island, offering stunning views and easy access to these iconic landmarks.

Activities

- **Waterfront Strolls**: Walk along the promenade while enjoying the fresh air and stunning views of New York Harbor.
- **Picnicking**: Bring a blanket and some snacks to relax in one of the many scenic spots within the park.
- **Cycling**: Rent a bike to explore the park's expansive trails.
- **Learning**: Stop by the Liberty Science Center to engage with hands-on science exhibits.

Insider Tips for Travelers

- **Read Carefully**: Always read the prompt and guidelines for the question carefully before beginning your response.
- **Plan Your Response**: For more extended responses, such as writing a memo or report, could you outline your main points before starting to write? This helps to organize thoughts and ensure that all relevant information is included.
- **Be Clear and Concise:** Avoid unnecessary words and jargon. Keep sentences short and to the point to ensure clarity.
- **Proofread**: Always check your writing for grammar and punctuation errors before submitting your response.

How to Get There

- **By Car**: Easily accessible via the New Jersey Turnpike, Exit 14B. Follow signs to Liberty State Park.
- **By Public Transport**: Take the PATH train to Exchange Place or Newport, then a short taxi or ride-share to the park.
- **By Ferry**: Some ferries from Manhattan dock directly at Liberty State Park, making it a convenient option for New York visitors.

Itinerary Suggestions :

Itinerary Type	Morning	Afternoon	Evening
Half-Day Visit	Take an early ferry to the Statue of Liberty and Ellis Island.	Stroll the promenade and enjoy a picnic in the park.	-
Full-Day Visit	Tour the Liberty Science Center.	Visit the Statue of Liberty and Ellis Island via ferry.	Watch the sunset over the Manhattan skyline.
Family-Friendly Visit	Explore the Liberty Science Center.	Enjoy a picnic lunch and walk or cycle along the trails.	-

Newark Museum of Art: A Cultural Treasure in New Jersey:

Why Visit?

The Newark Museum of Art is the largest museum in New Jersey, offering a blend of art, history, and interactive experiences. It's a must-visit for art lovers, families, and anyone seeking a cultural adventure.

Highlights

- **Extensive Art Collection:** Features American and decorative arts, a unique Tibetan collection, and rotating exhibits that highlight global cultures.
- **Planetarium:** Offers engaging shows that explore space and astronomy, perfect for both kids and adults.
- **The Ballantine House:** A stunningly restored Victorian mansion that provides a glimpse into 19th-century life.

Insider Tips for Travelers

- **Best Time to Visit:** Weekdays are quieter, making it easier to enjoy the exhibits and activities.
- **Family-Friendly:** MakerSPACE and the planetarium are perfect for kids, ensuring they stay engaged and entertained.

- **Photography:** While photography is allowed in some areas, check for restrictions, especially in special exhibits.
- **Dining:** There's a small café, but downtown Newark offers diverse dining options just a short walk away.

How to Get There

- **By Car**: Located at 49 Washington Street, Newark, NJ. Parking is available in nearby lots or on the street.
- **By Public Transport**: Take NJ Transit to Newark Penn Station, then a short walk or ride-share to the museum.
- **By Bus:** Local NJ Transit buses stop near the museum for easy access.

Itinerary Suggestions

Itinerary Type	Morning	Afternoon	Evening
Half-Day Visit	Explore the museum's main art collection.	Enjoy a planetarium show or visit MakerSPACE.	-
Full-Day Visit	Tour the museum exhibits, including the Ballantine House.	Attend a planetarium show and explore MakerSPACE.	Dine in downtown Newark.
Family-Friendly Visit	Visit MakerSPACE and the planetarium.	Tour the museum's American art collection.	-

The Newark Museum of Art

By Jim.henderson - Own work, CC BY-SA 4.0, https://commons.wikimedia.org/w/index.php?curid=88946776

New Jersey Performing Arts Center (NJPAC): A Hub of Culture in New Jersey

NJPAC is one of the most renowned performing arts venues in the U.S., offering a wide range of cultural experiences, from world-class concerts to local community events. Its vibrant atmosphere and diverse programming make it a cultural gem in New Jersey.

Highlights
- Top-Tier Productions: Hosts concerts, plays, Broadway-style shows, dance performances, jazz concerts, and comedy nights.
- Cultural Diversity: Celebrates global cultures with events and festivals that showcase music, art, and traditions from around the world.

Insider Tips for Travelers
- Arrive Early: The outdoor plaza often features live music, food trucks, and pre-show activities, enhancing the experience.
- Best Seats: For optimal views and sound, choose seats in the orchestra section or mezzanine.
- Dining Options: NJPAC is close to popular Newark eateries, offering cuisines from Italian to Portuguese. Consider dining before or after the show.
- Parking: On-site parking is available, but it's best to book in advance, especially during popular events.

New Jersey Performing Arts Center (NJPAC), Newark, New Jersey
By Kenneth C. Zirkel - Own work, CC BY-SA 4.0, https://commons.wikimedia.org/w/index.php?curid=116721294

Events

Check the NJPAC website for an updated schedule featuring:
- Broadway musicals and touring productions.
- Jazz and classical music concerts.
- Dance performances by world-renowned troupes.
- Stand-up comedy and spoken word events.

How to Get There

- **By Car:** Located at 1 Center Street, Newark, NJ. Parking garages and lots are available nearby.
- **By Public Transport:** NJ Transit trains to Newark Penn Station are just a 10-minute walk away.
- **By Bus:** NJ Transit buses frequently stop near the venue.

Itinerary Suggestions

Itinerary Type	Before the Show	Main Event	After the Show
Evening Visit	Explore the outdoor plaza with food trucks and live music.	Enjoy a concert, play, or performance at NJPAC.	Dine at a nearby restaurant or enjoy a drink at the outdoor plaza.
Daytime Event	Visit the nearby Newark Museum of Art.	Attend a matinee show or cultural event at NJPAC.	Stroll through Military Park or grab a coffee downtown.

Branch Brook Park (Cherry Blossoms)

Branch Brook Park is the nation's first county park, offering serene landscapes, historic architecture, and vibrant cherry blossoms in spring. Its tranquil beauty and variety of activities make it a top destination for nature lovers and families.

Highlights

- **Cherry Blossom Paradise:** Home to over 5,000 cherry blossom trees, more than Washington, D.C., making it a breathtaking springtime destination.
- **Historic Significance:** Designed by the Olmsted Brothers, renowned for creating New York's Central Park.
- **Expansive Grounds:** Spanning over 360 acres with scenic walking and biking trails, open fields, and lakes.

Cherry Blossom Festival

- **Timing:** Held annually in April during the cherry blossoms' peak bloom.
- **Events:** Enjoy cultural performances, family-friendly activities, and food vendors.
- **Tip:** Arrive early in the morning to beat the crowds and capture stunning photos.

Activities

Activity	Details
Jogging and Cycling	Scenic paths wind through the park, offering an enjoyable workout amidst nature.
Picnicking	Relax under the cherry blossoms with a packed lunch.
Photography	Capture breathtaking shots of the blossoms, especially during golden hour.
Seasonal Events	Participate in the Cherry Blossom 10K Run or family-friendly fun runs.

By User:EKoppel - Own work, Public Domain, https://commons.wikimedia.org/w/index.php?curid=18238184

By Jim.henderson - Own work, CC0, https://commons.wikimedia.org/w/index.php?curid=9878578

Insider Tips for Travelers

- Best Time to Visit: Peak bloom typically occurs in early to mid-April, but the park is beautiful year-round.
- Avoid Crowds: Visit on weekdays or early mornings during the Cherry Blossom Festival.
- Family-Friendly: Pack a picnic and enjoy the playgrounds and open spaces with kids.
- Accessibility: The park has several paved paths, making it wheelchair and stroller friendly.

How to Get There

- By Car: Enter via the main entrance at Park Avenue and Lake Street. Free parking is available throughout the park.
- By Public Transport: Take NJ Transit buses or the Newark Light Rail to Branch Brook Park Station.
- By Bike: The park is accessible via local bike trails and has plenty of space for cyclists.

Itinerary Suggestions

Itinerary Type	Morning	Afternoon	Evening
Half-Day Visit	Stroll through the cherry blossom groves.	Enjoy a picnic by the lake.	-
Full-Day Visit	Start with a jog or bike ride through the park.	Relax with lunch under the cherry blossoms.	Photograph the sunset over the scenic lake.
Family-Friendly Visit	Explore the trails and playgrounds.	Have a family picnic under the blossoms.	Enjoy a leisurely walk or take family photos.

(B) Hidden Gems

Thomas Edison's Menlo Park Museum: A Hidden Gem in New Jersey

Known as the "Birthplace of Modern Invention," Thomas Edison's Menlo Park Museum offers a fascinating glimpse into the life and legacy of one of the greatest inventors in history. It's a must-visit for science enthusiasts, history buffs, and families.

Highlights

- **Historic Significance**: Discover the site where Edison invented revolutionary technologies like the phonograph and perfected the electric light bulb.
- **Interactive Learning**: Engage with hands-on exhibits and models of Edison's inventions that showcase his ingenuity.
- **Recreated Labs**: Explore replicas of Edison's original Menlo Park laboratories, immersing yourself in the 19th-century inventor's environment.

Exhibits and Attractions

Artifacts on Display	View original tools, patents, and sketches used by Edison and his team.
Laboratory Recreation	Walk through Edison's meticulously recreated labs and learn how his experiments shaped modern life.
Interactive Displays	Try hands-on activities to understand the science behind Edison's inventions.

Insider Tips for Travelers

- **Best Time to Visit:** Weekdays are quieter, allowing for a more immersive experience.
- **Photography:** Bring a camera to capture the detailed recreations and historical artifacts.
- **Family-Friendly:** The museum offers engaging exhibits for children, making it an ideal educational outing.
- **Accessibility:** The museum is wheelchair accessible, ensuring everyone can enjoy the experience.

How to Get There

- **By Car**: Located off Route 27 in Edison, NJ, with free parking available onsite.
- **By Public Transport**: Take the NJ Transit train to Metuchen Station, followed by a short taxi or rideshare trip.
- **By Bike**: Accessible via local bike paths, with bike racks available near the museum.

Itinerary Suggestions

Itinerary Type	Morning	Afternoon	Evening
Half-Day Visit	Explore Edison's recreated laboratories.	Engage with interactive displays.	-
Full-Day Visit	Start with a guided tour of the museum.	Enjoy lunch at a nearby café.	Spend the evening at Roosevelt Park nearby.
Family-Friendly Visit	Dive into the interactive exhibits.	Participate in family-friendly workshops.	Relax with an outdoor stroll in Menlo Park.

The Edison Memorial Tower
By KForce at en.wikipedia, CC BY-SA 3.0,
https://commons.wikimedia.org/w/index.php?curid=17957520

Military Park: A Historic Gem in Newark

Military Park is a charming urban sanctuary blending rich history with vibrant modern culture. It offers visitors a peaceful escape amid the hustle and bustle of downtown Newark.

Highlights

- Historical Relevance: Once a Revolutionary War training ground, this park is steeped in American history.
- Sculptures and Art: Admire stunning statues like the Wars of America monument by Gutzon Borglum, the artist behind Mount Rushmore.
- Landscaped Beauty: Relax in the meticulously maintained gardens with seasonal blooms and tranquil fountains.

Features and Activities

Feature	Details
Outdoor Café	Enjoy seasonal treats and beverages with a view of the park's greenery.
Yoga Classes	Join free or low-cost yoga sessions for a refreshing start to your day.
Historic Sculptures	Discover art installations and monuments that highlight Newark's legacy.
Family-Friendly Events	Participate in activities like outdoor movie nights and pop-up markets.

Military Park
By Zeete - Own work, CC BY-SA 4.0,
https://commons.wikimedia.org/w/index.php?curid=116389341

Insider Tips for Travelers

- **Best Time to Visit:** Spring and summer afternoons are perfect for enjoying the gardens and outdoor events.
- **Photography Spot:** Capture beautiful shots of the fountain and the Wars of America statue.
- **Accessibility:** The park is wheelchair accessible, and nearby public transport makes it convenient to reach.
- **Local Vibe:** Visit during weekends to experience community gatherings and live music.

How to Get There

- **By Car**: Located at Broad Street and Park Place in Newark, with nearby parking garages available.
- **By Public Transport**: Take the NJ Transit train to Newark Penn Station, then walk 10 minutes to the park.
- **By Bike/Foot**: Easily accessible for cyclists and pedestrians from Newark's downtown area.

Itinerary Suggestions

Itinerary Type	Morning	Afternoon	Evening
Half-Day Visit	Explore the park's sculptures and gardens.	Relax with coffee at the outdoor café.	-
Full-Day Visit	Begin with a yoga class.	Stroll through the park and join a pop-up market.	Attend an outdoor movie or live performance.
Family-Friendly Visit	Walk through the park and enjoy the fountains.	Join a family activity or picnic.	End with a casual dinner at a nearby eatery.

(C) Activities in Gateway Region

Culinary Delights: Ironbound District, Newark, NJ

The Ironbound District in Newark is celebrated for its vibrant Portuguese and Brazilian culinary scene.

Dish Spotlight:

- **Bacalhau (Salted Cod)**: A Portuguese classic, often baked or grilled with potatoes and olives.
- **Feijoada (Brazilian Black Bean Stew)**: A hearty stew made with black beans and various meats, traditionally served with rice and collard greens.

Insider Tips:

- **Reservations**: Weekends can be busy; it's advisable to book ahead.
- **Parking**: Street parking is limited; consider using nearby parking garages or public transportation.
- **Cultural Experience**: Many restaurants feature live Fado music on weekends, enhancing the dining experience.

Sample Itineraries

1-Day Itinerary: Liberty and Lights

Time	Activity
Morning	Visit Liberty State Park for panoramic views of the Statue of Liberty and Manhattan skyline.
Afternoon	Attend a performance at the New Jersey Performing Arts Center (NJPAC).
Evening	Dine in the Ironbound District, savoring authentic Portuguese or Brazilian cuisine.

3-Day Itinerary: Exploring Newark's Treasures

Day	Morning	Afternoon	Evening
Day 1	Explore the Newark Museum of Art's diverse collections.	Participate in interactive exhibits and workshops.	Enjoy dinner at a local downtown restaurant.
Day 2	Stroll through Branch Brook Park, especially during cherry blossom season (April).	Have a picnic amidst the blooming trees.	Visit a local café for evening refreshments.
Day 3	Tour the Thomas Edison National Historical Park in West Orange.	Learn about Edison's inventions and explore his laboratory.	Return to Newark for an evening performance at NJPAC.

Gateway Region Highlights

Destination	Highlights	Best Time to Visit	Activities
Liberty State Park	Views of the Statue of Liberty and Manhattan skyline; waterfront promenade.	Year-round	Picnicking, walking, ferry rides.
Branch Brook Park	Over 5,000 cherry blossom trees; scenic parkland.	April (Cherry Blossom Festival)	Jogging, photography, picnics.
Newark Museum of Art	Extensive art collections; planetarium; Ballantine House.	Year-round	Museum tours, workshops, special exhibits.
New Jersey Performing Arts Center	Live performances, including Broadway shows and concerts.	Throughout the year	Theater, concerts, dining.
Thomas Edison National Historical Park	Edison's laboratories; historical exhibits.	Year-round	Historical tours, educational exhibits.

Tips for Your Gateway Region Adventure

- Check for Special Events: Consult local event calendars to discover festivals, concerts, and other happenings during your visit.
- Public Transportation: Utilize NJ Transit trains and buses for convenient travel within the region.
- Culinary Exploration: Sample diverse cuisines, from Portuguese and Brazilian in the Ironbound District to other international flavors throughout the area.
- Support Local Businesses: Visit boutiques, art galleries, and independent shops to contribute to the local economy.

7. The Ultimate New Jersey Travel Planner-150 Destinations

1. JERSEY SHORE GETAWAY: BEACHES, BOARDWALKS, AND FAMILY FUN (3 DAYS)

Day	Destination	Location	Activity	Time to Spend	Additional Info
1	Cape May Beach	Cape May	Relax on the beach, beachcombing	2-4 hours	Lifeguards available May-Sep; restrooms and changing facilities on-site.
1	Cape May Lighthouse	Cape May	Climb for stunning views	1 hour	Open daily May-Labor Day; fee applies; panoramic views of Atlantic and Delaware Bay.
1	Washington Street Mall	Cape May	Stroll and shop	2 hours	Pedestrian mall with unique shops, dining, and street performers in peak season.
2	Wildwood Boardwalk	Wildwood	Rides, games, dining	3-5 hours	Famous for tram cars, amusement piers, and diverse food options.
2	Morey's Piers	Wildwood	Amusement parks and waterparks	4-6 hours	Discounted combo tickets; thrilling rides, water slides, and arcades.
2	Sunset Beach	Cape May Point	Watch the sunset, mini-golf, explore shops	2 hours	Scenic sunsets, WWII bunker nearby, shops, and mini-golf for family fun.
3	Ocean City Boardwalk	Ocean City	Biking, arcade games, treats	3-4 hours	2.5-mile boardwalk with bike path, arcades, and classic boardwalk food.
3	Corson's Inlet State Park	Ocean City	Kayaking, fishing, hiking	2-3 hours	Kayak rentals, scenic fishing spots, and hiking trails with coastal views.
3	Jenkinson's Aquarium	Point Pleasant Beach	Marine life exhibits	1-2 hours	Features touch tanks and 1,500+ marine animals; ideal for young children.
3	Point Pleasant Beach	Point Pleasant Beach	Swimming, sunbathing, boardwalk fun	3-5 hours	Lifeguards during peak season; boardwalk entertainment and dining options.
Bonus	Barnegat Lighthouse State Park	Barnegat Light	Climb lighthouse, picnic	1-2 hours	Historic lighthouse with panoramic views; educational plaques; picnic areas.
Bonus	Seaside Heights Boardwalk	Seaside Heights	Rides, arcades, snacks	3-5 hours	Iconic boardwalk with lively rides, arcades, and the famous Kohr's Frozen Custard.
Bonus	Island Beach State Park	Seaside Park	Nature trails, fishing, swimming	3-4 hours	Hike/bike trails, birdwatching, fishing spots, and pristine beaches.
Bonus	Long Beach Island Beaches	Long Beach Island	Beach day, family surfing	4-5 hours	Gentle waves; surf lessons available; beach badges required in peak season.
Bonus	Fantasy Island Amusement Park	Long Beach Island	Rides, family arcade	2-3 hours	Family-friendly rides, arcades, and classic amusement park atmosphere.

2. FAMILY-FRIENDLY 5-DAY ITINERARY: EXPLORING NEW JERSEY'S BEST DESTINATIONS

Day	Destination	Location	Activity	Time to Spend	Additional Info
1	Liberty State Park	Jersey City	Picnic, hiking, skyline views	2-3 hours	Offers breathtaking views of Manhattan; picnic areas, walking trails, and ferry access to Ellis Island.
1	Liberty Science Center	Jersey City	Interactive exhibits and planetarium	2-4 hours	Great for families; features hands-on science exhibits and the largest planetarium in the Western Hemisphere.
1	Statue of Liberty (via ferry)	Jersey City/Ellis Island	Iconic landmark visit	3-4 hours	Ferry rides available; tickets include museum and crown access (book in advance).
2	Six Flags Great Adventure	Jackson	Thrill rides, safari park	Full day	Features roller coasters, kids' rides, and drive-through safari. Discounted tickets for online bookings.
2	Laurita Winery	New Egypt	Wine tasting, outdoor events	2-3 hours	Family-friendly events include food trucks and live music; non-alcoholic options for kids.
2	Grounds for Sculpture	Hamilton	Art exhibits, outdoor sculptures	3-4 hours	Stunning outdoor art installations; family-friendly, with dining options available on-site.
3	Princeton University	Princeton	Campus tour, historic sites	1-2 hours	Explore the historic Ivy League campus and notable architecture.
3	Princeton Art Museum	Princeton	Art collections, exhibitions	1-2 hours	Free admission; diverse art collections spanning ancient to contemporary works.
3	Delaware and Raritan Canal	Princeton	Kayaking, walking, or biking	2-3 hours	Scenic trail along the canal; ideal for outdoor enthusiasts.
4	Adventure Aquarium	Camden	Explore marine life exhibits	3-4 hours	Features a shark tunnel, hippos, and interactive touch tanks; great for kids.
4	Battleship New Jersey Museum	Camden	Tour the historic battleship	2-3 hours	Self-guided and guided tours available; learn about WWII naval history.
4	Cooper River Park	Pennsauken	Biking, boating, picnic	2-3 hours	Features a lake for paddle boating, biking trails, and picnic areas.
5	Thomas Edison National Park	West Orange	Tour Edison's laboratory and home	1-2 hours	Learn about Edison's inventions through interactive exhibits; admission fee applies.
5	Turtle Back Zoo	West Orange	Zoo visit, carousel, and playground	2-4 hours	Family-friendly zoo with a variety of animal exhibits; mini-golf and train rides available.
5	South Mountain Reservation	West Orange	Hiking, waterfalls, scenic views	2-3 hours	Offers diverse trails for all levels, picnic areas, and stunning natural scenery.

3. ADVENTURE AND NATURE ESCAPADE: 5-DAY ITINERARY ACROSS NEW JERSEY

Day	Destination	Location	Activity	Time to Spend	Additional Info
1	Delaware Water Gap National Recreation Area	Northwest NJ	Hiking, kayaking, and wildlife spotting	4-6 hours	Features stunning trails like the Mt. Tammany hike. Kayak rentals available. Ideal for outdoor enthusiasts.
1	Dingmans Falls	Delaware Water Gap	Waterfall viewing, nature photography	1-2 hours	Easy access via a short trail. Second highest waterfall in PA, near NJ border.
1	Millbrook Village	Hardwick Township	Step back into a 19th-century village	1-2 hours	Offers guided tours and live demonstrations of historical crafts during special events.
2	High Point State Park	Sussex	Scenic views, hiking, and picnicking	3-5 hours	Features NJ's highest elevation with views of three states. Visitor center and picnic spots available.
2	Sussex County Sunflower Maze	Sandyston	Walk through vibrant sunflower fields	1-2 hours	Seasonal attraction (late summer). Great for photography and family fun.
2	Space Farms Zoo & Museum	Sussex	Wildlife exhibits and historic artifacts	2-3 hours	Home to over 500 animals and a fascinating museum showcasing antique cars and tools.
3	Paterson Great Falls National Historical Park	Paterson	View waterfalls and learn local history	1-2 hours	Guided tours available. Visit the nearby museum to learn about Paterson's industrial heritage.
3	Garrett Mountain Reservation	Woodland Park	Hiking, birdwatching, and picnicking	2-3 hours	Offers sweeping views of NYC. Popular for birdwatching and serene walking trails.
3	Lambert Castle Museum	Paterson	Explore history and unique exhibits	1-2 hours	Built in 1892, this castle offers stunning architecture and local historical displays.
4	Grounds for Sculpture	Hamilton Township	Explore art installations in nature	3-4 hours	A 42-acre park blending art and landscape design. On-site café and guided tours available.
4	Sayen House and Gardens	Hamilton Township	Stroll through themed gardens	1-2 hours	Known for its seasonal blooms. Free entry and ideal for a relaxing afternoon.
4	Mercer Lake	West Windsor Township	Boating, kayaking, and fishing	2-3 hours	Boat rentals available seasonally. Great for families who enjoy water activities.
5	Liberty Science Center	Jersey City	Interactive science exhibits	3-4 hours	Features IMAX theaters and hands-on exhibits for all ages. Book tickets online for a smoother experience.
5	Liberty State Park	Jersey City	Walk along the waterfront, picnicking	2-3 hours	Offers stunning views of the Statue of Liberty and NYC skyline. Ideal for family picnics.
5	Hudson River Waterfront Walkway	Jersey City to Hoboken	Scenic walk along the waterfront	1-2 hours	Enjoy a leisurely stroll or bike ride with views of Manhattan. Plenty of dining options along the way.

4. HISTORY AND HERITAGE TRAIL: 4-DAY JOURNEY THROUGH NEW JERSEY'S RICH PAST

Day	Destination	Location	Activity	Time to Spend	Additional Info
1	Princeton University Campus	Princeton	Explore historic architecture and art	2-3 hours	Free self-guided tours available. Don't miss the Princeton University Art Museum.
1	Morven Museum & Garden	Princeton	Learn about NJ's colonial history	1-2 hours	Former governor's mansion with exhibits on NJ history and culture.
1	Battlefield State Park	Princeton	Walk through Revolutionary War history	2-3 hours	Offers guided tours and interpretive signage. Great for history buffs and nature lovers.
2	Thomas Edison National Historical Park	West Orange	Visit Edison's laboratory and home	2-3 hours	Discover where Edison developed groundbreaking inventions. Guided tours and hands-on exhibits available.
2	Grover Cleveland Birthplace	Caldwell	Explore the home of the 22nd & 24th president	1-2 hours	Small but informative museum with artifacts from Cleveland's life and presidency.
2	Millburn Township Historic District	Millburn	Stroll through historic architecture	1-2 hours	Features preserved homes and buildings dating back to the 18th century.
3	Ellis Island Immigration Museum	Jersey City	Discover immigrant stories and history	3-4 hours	Accessible via ferry. Combine with a visit to the Statue of Liberty.
3	Red Bank Battlefield Park	National Park	Revolutionary War battlefield site	2-3 hours	Offers walking trails and monuments. Learn about the 1777 Battle of Red Bank.
3	Indian King Tavern Museum	Haddonfield	Tour a historic colonial tavern	1-2 hours	Important site where NJ's statehood was declared. Guided tours available.
4	Cape May Historic District	Cape May	Tour Victorian-era homes and streets	3-4 hours	Take a trolley tour for an immersive experience. Visit the Emlen Physick Estate for a glimpse into the past.
4	Naval Air Station Wildwood Aviation Museum	Cape May	Explore historic aircraft	2-3 hours	Features WWII-era planes and hands-on exhibits for families.
4	Wheaton Arts and Cultural Center	Millville	Watch glassblowing demonstrations	2-3 hours	Unique venue showcasing glass art and NJ's artisan heritage.

5. NATURE'S ESCAPE: A 4-DAY ADVENTURE IN NEW JERSEY'S GREAT OUTDOORS

Day	Destination	Location	Activity	Time to Spend	Additional Info
1	Delaware Water Gap National Recreation Area	Columbia	Hiking, kayaking, scenic views	4-5 hours	Offers trails of varying difficulty and breathtaking views of the Delaware River.
1	Buttermilk Falls	Walpack Township	Short hike to a picturesque waterfall	1-2 hours	Easy access to one of NJ's most beautiful waterfalls. Perfect for families with young children.
1	Lakota Wolf Preserve	Columbia	Observe wolves in a natural habitat	1-2 hours	Guided tours available. Reservations required.
2	High Point State Park	Sussex County	Hiking, swimming, and panoramic views	3-4 hours	Home to NJ's highest point. Don't miss the High Point Monument.
2	Stokes State Forest	Branchville	Camping, fishing, and nature trails	3-4 hours	Great for outdoor enthusiasts. Offers family-friendly picnic areas.
2	Space Farms Zoo and Museum	Sussex	Zoo and antique museum	2-3 hours	Features over 100 species of animals and historic artifacts.
3	Liberty State Park	Jersey City	Picnicking, hiking, and waterfront views	3-4 hours	Offers a stunning view of Manhattan and the Statue of Liberty. Ideal for a family day outdoors.
3	Meadowlands Environmental Center	Lyndhurst	Explore wetlands and wildlife	2-3 hours	Interactive exhibits and walking trails for kids and nature lovers.
3	Hacklebarney State Park	Long Valley	Hiking and trout fishing	2-3 hours	Known for scenic beauty with streams and wooden bridges. Great for photography enthusiasts.
4	Pine Barrens	Southern NJ	Canoeing, birdwatching, and hiking	3-5 hours	Unique ecosystem. Consider the Batsto River for a canoeing adventure.
4	Atlantic County Park at Estell Manor	Estell Manor	Nature trails and historic ruins	2-3 hours	Features a blend of history and nature. Enjoy easy walking trails through lush surroundings.
4	Edwin B. Forsythe National Wildlife Refuge	Oceanville	Birdwatching and wildlife photography	2-3 hours	One of the best spots in NJ for birdwatching. Seasonal events for families and kids.

6. CULTURAL GEMS AND HISTORICAL TRAILS: A 3-DAY JOURNEY THROUGH NEW JERSEY'S HERITAGE

Day	Destination	Location	Activity	Time to Spend	Additional Info
1	Princeton University Campus	Princeton	Campus tour, architecture walk	2-3 hours	Explore historic buildings and beautiful gardens. Free self-guided tours available.
1	Princeton University Art Museum	Princeton	View renowned art collections	1-2 hours	Admission is free. Family-friendly exhibits available.
1	Morven Museum & Garden	Princeton	Tour the historic mansion and garden	1-2 hours	Former NJ governor's mansion. Offers rotating exhibits and guided tours.
2	Liberty Science Center	Jersey City	Interactive exhibits and planetarium shows	3-4 hours	Perfect for families. Features the largest planetarium in the Western Hemisphere.
2	Ellis Island Immigration Museum	Jersey City	Learn about immigration history	2-3 hours	Accessible by ferry. Combine with a visit to the Statue of Liberty for a full day of history.
2	Red Mill Museum Village	Clinton	Explore historic buildings and exhibits	1-2 hours	Picturesque location along the Raritan River. Perfect for photography enthusiasts.
3	Thomas Edison National Historical Park	West Orange	Discover Edison's laboratory and home	2-3 hours	Guided tours provide an in-depth look at Edison's inventions and legacy.
3	Paterson Great Falls National Historical Park	Paterson	View historic falls and industrial history	2-3 hours	Offers a glimpse into the early industrial era of America.
3	Lambert Castle	Paterson	Explore a historic home with scenic views	1-2 hours	Museum inside offers exhibits on local history.
3	Grounds For Sculpture	Hamilton	Outdoor art exhibits and sculptures	2-4 hours	Combines nature and art in an immersive experience. Family-friendly trails and dining options available.

7. NATURE ESCAPES AND OUTDOOR ADVENTURES: A 3-DAY EXPEDITION THROUGH NEW JERSEY'S WILD SIDE

Day	Destination	Location	Activity	Time to Spend	Additional Info
1	Delaware Water Gap National Recreation Area	Northwest NJ	Hiking, kayaking, scenic views	4-6 hours	Features over 100 miles of trails, including the Appalachian Trail. Water activities available seasonally.
	Buttermilk Falls	Walpack Township	Short hike to a stunning waterfall	1-2 hours	Easy-access trails make it family-friendly. Best visited after rainfall for maximum water flow.
	Lakota Wolf Preserve	Columbia	Guided wolf tours and nature photography	1-2 hours	Reservations required. Learn about conservation efforts and observe wolves in their natural habitat.
2	High Point State Park	Sussex County	Scenic hiking, picnic, and monument visit	2-4 hours	Home to New Jersey's highest point. Offers panoramic views of three states.
	Stokes State Forest	Branchville	Camping, hiking, and wildlife spotting	2-4 hours	A great spot for birdwatching and beginner-friendly trails.
	Kittatinny Valley State Park	Andover	Biking, boating, and fishing	3-4 hours	Trails suitable for all skill levels. Seasonal rentals available for boating and biking.
3	Duke Farms	Hillsborough Township	Nature trails, sustainable gardening exhibits	3-4 hours	Features eco-friendly practices and educational programs. Free entry, but donations are welcome.
	Great Swamp National Wildlife Refuge	Morris County	Wildlife observation and nature photography	2-3 hours	Boardwalks and trails provide easy access for families. Bring binoculars for birdwatching.
	Hacklebarney State Park	Chester Township	Scenic trails and picnic spots	2-3 hours	Known for its beautiful fall foliage and tranquil environment.
	Sourland Mountain Preserve	Somerset County	Hiking and rock climbing	2-4 hours	Offers trails with varying difficulty and boulder fields for climbing enthusiasts.

8. HISTORIC GEMS AND CULTURAL HIGHLIGHTS: A 3-DAY JOURNEY THROUGH NEW JERSEY'S RICH HERITAGE

Day	Destination	Location	Activity	Time to Spend	Additional Info
1	Liberty State Park	Jersey City	Visit the park and view the Manhattan skyline	2-3 hours	Offers ferry access to the Statue of Liberty and Ellis Island. Free entry to the park; ferry tickets extra.
1	Ellis Island Immigration Museum	Jersey City	Explore immigration history	2-3 hours	Guided and self-guided tours available. Ferry departs from Liberty State Park.
1	Statue of Liberty	Jersey City	Tour the statue and museum	2-3 hours	Reservations recommended for pedestal or crown access.
2	Princeton University	Princeton	Campus tour, art museum	2-3 hours	Offers free guided tours. Don't miss the Princeton University Art Museum.
2	Morven Museum & Garden	Princeton	Explore history and gardens	1-2 hours	Former New Jersey governor's mansion. Features rotating exhibits and historic artifacts.
2	Drumthwacket	Princeton	Visit the governor's residence	1-2 hours	Tours available by appointment. Historic site showcasing New Jersey governance.
3	Thomas Edison National Historical Park	West Orange	Explore Edison's lab and inventions	2-3 hours	Learn about Edison's contributions to modern technology. Admission fees apply.
3	Paterson Great Falls	Paterson	Visit historic falls and industrial park	2-3 hours	Offers insight into New Jersey's industrial revolution. Guided tours available.
3	Lambert Castle	Paterson	Museum showcasing local history	1-2 hours	Features artifacts, historic furniture, and art. Located near Paterson Great Falls.
3	Grounds for Sculpture	Hamilton	Art and sculpture park	3-4 hours	Outdoor art exhibits in a beautifully landscaped environment. Admission fee required.

9. FAMILY-FRIENDLY ADVENTURES: A 3-DAY FUN-FILLED ITINERARY IN NEW JERSEY

Day	Destination	Location	Activity	Time to Spend	Additional Info
1	Adventure Aquarium	Camden	Explore marine life and interactive exhibits	3-4 hours	Features shark tunnels, hippos, and touch tanks. Family-friendly dining options available on-site.
1	Battleship New Jersey	Camden	Tour the historic battleship	2-3 hours	Guided and self-guided tours available. Family scavenger hunts offered.
1	Camden Children's Garden	Camden	Play areas and garden exploration	1-2 hours	Includes themed gardens, butterfly house, and kid-friendly activities.
2	Turtle Back Zoo	West Orange	Visit animals, ride train, carousel	3-4 hours	Features a mini-golf course, treetop adventure park, and zoo-themed playground.
2	South Mountain Reservation	West Orange	Hiking, picnicking, and scenic views	2-3 hours	Offers trails of varying difficulty and picnic areas. Great for outdoor family fun.
2	Imagine That! Children's Museum	Florham Park	Hands-on exhibits and creative play	2-3 hours	Focused on children under 8. Features STEM activities, art spaces, and pretend play zones.
3	Six Flags Great Adventure	Jackson	Amusement park rides and attractions	Full day	Offers a variety of rides for all ages. Includes family-friendly dining and entertainment options.
3	Six Flags Safari	Jackson	Drive-through wildlife safari	1-2 hours	Encounter over 1,200 animals in a 350-acre reserve. Tickets can be bundled with Six Flags admission.
3	Allaire State Park	Wall Township	Explore historic village and train rides	2-3 hours	Includes a living history museum and seasonal events. Great for young children.
3	Jersey Shore Pirates	Brick	Pirate-themed boat adventure for kids	1-2 hours	Interactive sailing adventure with costumes and treasure hunts. Advance reservations recommended.

10. NEW JERSEY HIDDEN GEMS: 3-DAY ITINERARY FOR UNIQUE AND OFF-THE-BEATEN-PATH EXPERIENCES

Day	Destination	Location	Activity	Time to Spend	Additional Info
1	Grounds for Sculpture	Hamilton Township	Explore sculptures and art exhibits	3-4 hours	A 42-acre park with over 270 sculptures. Beautiful gardens, perfect for photography.
1	Sayen Gardens	Hamilton Township	Walk through lush gardens	1-2 hours	Offers seasonal flower displays. Best visited during spring and fall.
1	Princeton University Art Museum	Princeton	Explore art exhibits from around the world	1-2 hours	Free admission. Features diverse collections, from ancient to modern art.
2	Paterson Great Falls National Historical Park	Paterson	Visit the falls and learn about the history	2-3 hours	Historic site offering scenic views of the Great Falls. Great for photography and educational tours.
2	Lambert Castle	Paterson	Tour the historic castle and its museum	1-2 hours	Offers educational exhibits and beautiful views of the surrounding area.
2	The New Jersey Botanical Garden	Ringwood	Stroll through themed gardens	2-3 hours	Includes formal gardens, woodlands, and beautiful trails for a peaceful experience.
3	Hoboken Waterfront	Hoboken	Walk along the waterfront, enjoy city views	2-3 hours	Enjoy stunning views of Manhattan. Great for photo ops, dining, and relaxing.
3	Liberty Landing Marina	Jersey City	Explore waterfront dining and shops	2-3 hours	Dining options with views of the Statue of Liberty and the Manhattan skyline.
3	Skylands Manor	Ringwood	Explore the mansion and gardens	1-2 hours	Historic manor with themed gardens. Best for those interested in history and peaceful escapes.

Appendix

97

MUST-VISIT RESTAURANTS/EATING PLACES IN NEW JERSEY

Restaurant	Location	Why Visit
Good Karma Cafe	Asbury Park	Vegan comfort food with a creative, plant-based menu.
Toki	Hackensack	High-quality Japanese cuisine, known for sushi and authentic dishes.
Semolina	Metuchen	Farm-to-table eatery featuring seasonal, locally sourced ingredients.
Caterina	Red Bank	Fine Italian dining steps from the scenic Navesink River.
Monticello	Red Bank	Warm atmosphere with classic Italian dishes and excellent reviews.
JBJ Soul Kitchen	Red Bank	A community-focused eatery by Jon Bon Jovi, serving delicious food while giving back.
Patrizia's	Red Bank	Upscale Italian cuisine in an elegant and inviting setting.
Teak Asian Fusion	Morristown	Unique Asian flavors combined in a creative fusion menu.
Char	Hasbrouck Heights	Incredible steakhouse ideal for special occasions.
Buona Sera	Red Bank	Beloved Italian restaurant with a warm ambiance and classic menu.
Scarborough Fair	Sea Girt	Stunning seafood dishes served with beautiful ocean views.
Moonstruck	Asbury Park	Gorgeous seasonal menu and a charming atmosphere.
Rooney's Oceanfront Restaurant	Long Branch	Waterfront dining with stunning views and fresh seafood.

Additional New Jersey Dining Facts

- **Diners:** New Jersey is famous for its diners, offering classic comfort food all day long (e.g., Tops Diner).

- **Pork Roll**: New Jersey claims the invention of the pork roll (also known as Taylor Ham), a popular breakfast staple.

- **Pizza**: Known for regional pizza variations, including the thin-crust tomato pie from De Lorenzo's.

MUST-VISIT KID-FRIENDLY SITES IN NEW JERSEY

Attraction	Location	Why Visit
Cape May County Zoo	Cape May Court House	Free admission, home to over 550 animals, and includes a large playground and picnic areas.
Adventure Aquarium	Camden	Features unique exhibits like a shark tunnel, hippos, and interactive touch tanks.
Turtle Back Zoo	West Orange	Offers a wide variety of animals, a train ride, playground, and even a treetop adventure course.
Jenkinson's Aquarium	Point Pleasant Beach	Small, kid-friendly aquarium with seals, penguins, and touch tanks.
Liberty Science Center	Jersey City	Hands-on science exhibits, a planetarium, and educational activities perfect for kids.
Van Saun County Park	Paramus	Includes a zoo, train rides, carousel, playgrounds, and picnic areas.
Grounds for Sculpture	Hamilton	A unique sculpture park that blends art and nature, with plenty of open space for kids to explore.
Six Flags Great Adventure & Safari	Jackson	A combination of an amusement park and a drive-through safari adventure featuring wild animals.
Storybook Land	Egg Harbor Township	A fairy tale-themed amusement park with gentle rides and activities for younger children.
Field Station: Dinosaurs	Leonia	An outdoor dinosaur-themed park featuring life-size animatronic dinosaurs and interactive shows.
Fosterfields Living Historical Farm	Morristown	A working historical farm where kids can learn about early 20th-century farming and interact with animals.
Branch Brook Park	Newark	Known for its beautiful cherry blossoms in spring, with open spaces for picnics and play.
Wildwoods Boardwalk and Beach	Wildwood	Family-friendly boardwalk with rides, games, and free beaches ideal for kids of all ages.

SEASONAL FESTIVALS IN NEW JERSEY

Festival Name	Season	Location	Why Visit
New Jersey Seafood Festival	Spring	Belmar	Enjoy fresh seafood, live music, and family-friendly activities along the waterfront.
QuickChek New Jersey Festival of Ballooning	Summer	Readington	Witness breathtaking hot air balloons, live concerts, and food vendors in this vibrant festival.
Chatsworth Cranberry Festival	Fall	Chatsworth	Celebrate the cranberry harvest with crafts, food, and live entertainment in the Pine Barrens.
Holiday in the Park (Six Flags)	Winter	Jackson	Experience Six Flags transformed with festive lights, holiday rides, and seasonal performances.
Lighthouse International Film Festival	Summer	Long Beach Island	Perfect for movie enthusiasts, showcasing independent films in a beachside setting.
Atlantic City Beer and Music Festival	Spring	Atlantic City	Combines craft beer tastings with live music for a lively, fun-filled event.
Cowtown Rodeo and Flea Market	Summer	Pilesgrove	Enjoy authentic rodeo events alongside one of New Jersey's largest flea markets.

BEST SEASONAL ATTRACTIONS FOR FAMILIES

Attraction	Season	Why Visit
Rutgers Gardens	Spring	Gorgeous flower displays and walking paths; perfect for a family picnic in bloom.
Wildwoods Morey's Piers	Summer	Family-friendly amusement park with rides, games, and water parks along the boardwalk.
Terhune Orchards	Fall	Apple and pumpkin picking, hayrides, and seasonal farm activities for families.
Skylands Stadium Christmas Light Show	Winter	A festive drive-through light show with holiday-themed displays and family-friendly activities.

TOP HISTORICAL SITES FOR FAMILIES IN NEW JERSEY

Attraction	Location	Why Visit
Ellis Island and Liberty State Park	Jersey City	Take a ferry to explore Ellis Island and the Statue of Liberty, combining history with a fun boat ride.
Historic Cold Spring Village	Cape May	A living history museum with interactive exhibits and costumed interpreters showcasing 19th-century life.
Princeton Battlefield State Park	Princeton	Learn about Revolutionary War history with open grounds perfect for picnics and exploration.

BEST ADVENTURE ACTIVITIES FOR FAMILIES

Activity	Location	Why Visit
The Delaware River Tubing	Frenchtown	A relaxing tubing adventure with beautiful scenery and a floating food stop along the way.
Diggerland USA	West Berlin	A construction-themed amusement park where kids can operate real construction machinery.
Cape May Whale Watcher	Cape May	Offers exciting whale and dolphin watching tours on the Atlantic Ocean.

BEST SEASONAL ATTRACTIONS FOR FAMILIES

Attraction	Season	Why Visit
Rutgers Gardens	Spring	Gorgeous flower displays and walking paths; perfect for a family picnic in bloom.
Wildwoods Morey's Piers	Summer	Family-friendly amusement park with rides, games, and water parks along the boardwalk.
Terhune Orchards	Fall	Apple and pumpkin picking, hayrides, and seasonal farm activities for families.
Skylands Stadium Christmas Light Show	Winter	A festive drive-through light show with holiday-themed displays and family-friendly activities.

CONCLUSION: EMBRACE THE SPIRIT OF NEW JERSEY ADVENTURE

As you close this guidebook, remember that New Jersey is far more than its reputation. It's a state where natural beauty meets rich history, vibrant cities coexist with serene landscapes, and every corner holds a new story waiting to be discovered. From the rugged trails of the Ridge and Valley to the pristine beaches of the Atlantic Coastal Plain, New Jersey offers a unique adventure for every kind of traveler.

Whether you're seeking relaxation, family fun, outdoor thrills, or a cultural deep dive, the Garden State promises an experience that will stay with you long after your journey ends. Let its diverse regions inspire you to step off the beaten path, uncover hidden gems, and create unforgettable memories with your loved ones.

Use the itineraries, insider tips, and resources in this book to make your exploration seamless and fulfilling. Don't forget to savor the local flavors, immerse yourself in the seasonal festivals, and learn from the stories etched into the state's landmarks.

New Jersey is a place of boundless discovery. So pack your bags, set your itinerary—or let serendipity guide you—and embark on the adventure of a lifetime. The Garden State awaits!
Safe travels and happy exploring!

www.ingramcontent.com/pod-product-compliance
Lightning Source LLC
Chambersburg PA
CBHW081403070526
44583CB00020B/2662